SYSTEMS OF HIGHER EDUCATION: UNITED STATES

Alan Pifer
John Shea
David Henry
Lyman Glenny

I|C International Council for Educational Development
E|D

Copyright © 1978 by International Council for Educational Development

ISBN Number: 0-89192-210-5

Printed in the United States of America

Distributed by Interbook Inc., 13 East 16th Street, New York, N.Y. 10003

CONTENTS

FOREWORD	v
Introduction: Some Current Issues Alan Pifer	1
Design and Function John R. Shea	19
Administration of Higher Education David D. Henry	51
Effectiveness of the System Lyman A. Glenny	81
LIST OF COUNTRY DIRECTORS	131

FOREWORD

An important and largely unexamined development in higher education is the emergence of systems of institutions, which are planned and managed by advisory, coordinating, or governing bodies poised between institutions and governments. Countries with highly centralized governments now seek to devolve responsibility on such organizations, while in other countries the effort is to move from individual autonomous institutions to more central planning and controls. In both cases, a balance is sought between the values of institutional independence and public responsibility. Problems of organization and procedure are similar but patterns of solution vary widely. The design and management of the systems are, therefore, of universal interest and merit comparative study.

The central issue is easy to state but extremely difficult to answer: How can systems of higher education be designed and managed so as to assure maximum flexibility for institutions with responsible monitoring of the public interest?

Everywhere on the international scene, institutions of higher education are seeing their autonomy challenged—their right to decide their own methods of operation in management, in teaching, and in setting their own goals and purposes. Whether the institutions are public or private, this independence is directly threatened. Public funds and planning call for accountability and service in the national interest as government and society may see it.

The International Council for Educational Development has, for some years, watched this development. It produced what was, to our knowledge, the first collection of essays on the subject in 1972 under the title *Higher Education: From Autonomy to Systems*. So we welcomed the opportunity provided through a generous grant from the Krupp Foundation of the Federal Republic of Germany to make a three-year comparative analysis of how different countries are adjusting their higher education systems to meet the new demands.

Twelve countries were invited to participate. Guidelines were given for the study with the admonition that they were not to be inflexibly followed: each country needed latitude to explain its own context, development, and unique characteristics. Some problems would be more pertinent to one country than another. Further, we asked for a frank evaluation. Aside from the first section requesting a description of the system with data on institutions, enrollment, and various patterns of governance, the body of each study rests on the informed opinion of leaders in the higher education of the country.

In this respect the study differs from many preceding efforts to draw comparisons based on quantifiable facts. Seldom has that approach yielded more than a collection of data presented in a series of separate descriptions. So we have endeavored to go one step further and provide critical analysis of the issues being faced and the solutions being tried.

The study, in its entirety, comprises: twelve books, one for each country; a volume, crossing national lines, which explores the five major topics selected for analysis—planning, administration, and management; coordination; effectiveness of the system in meeting its social purposes; the effectiveness of the system to change and adjust; and the efficiency of the system—and finally, there is a concluding report.

On a broad scale this study offers a statement about how different countries are dealing with critical problems of educational planning and operations. It speaks to social scientists and public officials who are necessarily concerned with problems of social unrest and cohesion as well as finance and changing priorities. It further holds the prospect of learning from the experience of others. Most educational systems have imported ideas from abroad, or at least they have been stimulated frequently by others to think creatively about their own systems. Also the study provides the means to learn of others' successes as well as difficulties. Finally, there is the possibility of discovering some general rules of governance that should be studied carefully by all those concerned with macroplanning of higher education.

We urge a careful reading of this study on the United States. It will be enlightening to the intracountry audience as a comment on their present situation. For interested parties in other countries, it is a critique that will illuminate their own efforts and stage of development. And those working at the frontier of international comparative studies in higher education will discover, we trust, a valuable piece in an international puzzle.

To present the picture in the United States, we invited John Shea of the Carnegie Council on Policy Studies in Higher Education to describe the chief characteristics; David Henry, president-emeritus of the University of Illinois at Urbana to discuss issues of management and administration; and Lyman Glenny, former director of the Center for Research in Higher Education at Berkeley to report on the effectiveness of our higher education systems. In order to emphasize current problems we have added a statement by Alan Pifer, president of the Carnegie Corporation of New York. We are most indebted to these gentlemen for their outstanding contribution to this study.

February 1978   James A. Perkins
                                                   Nell P. Eurich

INTRODUCTION: SOME CURRENT ISSUES*

Alan Pifer

I propose to discuss four major issues of current concern in American higher education: access, the needs of youth, the preservation of elitism, and institutional autonomy. None of these issues is unique to the United States. They are already in evidence or are at least incipient in virtually all systems of higher education in the world.

Access

Broadly, the issue of access can be posed in the questions: For whom should higher education be available and who should make that decision — individuals, institutions, governments, the courts, or some combination of the four? Underlying this issue is a philosophical question concerning the very nature of higher education. What is it essentially? Is it a constitutional or other basic human right? Is it a commodity to be purchased in the marketplace? Or is it a form of social and economic investment, to be determined by the state?

Here in the United States we define higher education in all of these seemingly incompatible ways, with consequent tension in the system and within individual institutions, the cause of which is not always clearly understood. Fortunately, however, our large and highly diversified system, with its many centers of power and initiative and the wide choice it offers students, allows the consequences of a pluralistic definition of higher education to be played out with a minimum of open confrontation. Only occasionally, as

---

*This statement comes from an address presented to the Conference of Commonwealth Vice-Chancellors at Aspen, Colorado, September 7, 1976.

presently in the City University of New York, do the conflicting ideologies and their implications become sharply enough identified to make the nature of the tension clear to the public.

For most of its history American higher education, despite its much vaunted land grant colleges, was not a very democratic enterprise. If you were poor, black, Spanish-speaking, native American Indian, female, or physically handicapped, your chances of participating in it equally—as students, faculty members, or administrators—were extremely limited. It is only in the past decade, as the result of constitutional tests in the courts more than two decades ago and subsequent civil rights legislation and presidential executive orders, that our colleges and universities have opened their doors on something like an equal basis to all citizens.

This does not yet mean that every deserving person can get through those doors. What ought to be irrelevant factors—poverty, race, sex, and even the location of one's home—still have some effect on one's chances in higher education. Deliberate, overt discrimination, however, is no longer the primary cause of lower participation by some groups; more important is the actual availability of qualified individuals to participate. The effects of past discrimination and the continuing impact of poverty and racially segregated housing on the quality of lower levels of schooling clearly limit the capacity of some Americans to compete equally in all aspects of higher education.

Nevertheless, we unquestionably have come a long way in recent years toward expanding higher educational opportunity for all. This has been accomplished through a new sense of social conscience which arose generally in academic institutions in the 1960s, through governmental pressure, through the militancy of excluded groups, through new programs of student assistance (such as the Federal Basic Opportunity Grants), and through widespread construction of low-cost, open access, two-year community colleges. We have, furthermore, tried to make good the effects of past discrimination by giving those groups which have been its victims various forms of special consideration.

"Affirmative action," as this policy of compensation for the past wrongs is called, has, indeed, become a matter of sharp public dispute. Many Americans believe that we have now come far enough in ensuring equal opportunity simply by making discrimination illegal. They do not support the idea of special treatment for minorities and women, either in higher education or elsewhere in our national life. They maintain that the goals established by affirmative action plans are in reality quotas and, consequently, represent a reimposition of discrimination, this time against white males. A number of cases challenging affirmative action have been brought to the courts, thus far with inconclusive results, in the sense that no case with broad applicability has yet been decided by the Supreme Court. The celebrated *de Funis* case, the only one the Court has heard, was declared moot on technical grounds.[1]

Other Americans, with whom I count myself, believe that if affirmative action were to be abandoned at this stage, some of the gains made by minorities and women might well be lost, and certainly there would be little additional progress for them.

The sad truth is that, with a few exceptions, American higher education throughout more than three centuries of existence did virtually nothing to promote equality of opportunity and moved finally only when it was forced. Given the opportunity, most institutions would no doubt gradually relax their efforts, especially their efforts to hire and, in due course, promote to tenured or senior positions more minority group members and women for their faculties and administrative staffs. I will come back to the rather special matter of the *way* the federal affirmative action program in higher education is administered when I discuss the issue of institutional autonomy.

Debate over discrimination against women, the handicapped, and specific racial, linguistic, ethnic, or tribal groups, although highly important not only in the United States but in most countries of the world, approaches the issue of access to higher education somewhat narrowly. A broader way is to consider what proportion of young people generally *should* be provided postsecondary educational opportunity and, within that group, what numbers should be admitted to universities and what to other types of institutions.

Due to the diversity of our higher educational system and its pluralistic control by the fifty states and numerous private authorities, these questions have never received quite the same sharp focus they have had in countries with unitary central government control of higher education. Nevertheless, today we do have a kind of national "policy," or at least consensus, on the matter of access. This policy, which is of course the aggregate of a variety of federal, state, and even local decisions, is to provide a place in higher education for any young person who successfully completes high school. Implementation of the policy has been heavily dependent on the construction of two-year community colleges by the states, joined in some cases by local authorities. Between 1963-1970 the number of these institutions almost doubled and their enrollments nearly tripled.

Despite a national commitment to universal access, as just defined, doubts have arisen in the past few years as to just how many high school leavers *should* go on to higher education at that point of their lives. I will discuss this further in connection with my second topic, the needs of youth.

Still another way to consider access has come to the forefront in the country recently. Historically, higher education was almost exclusively thought of as an activity reserved for young people eighteen to twenty-one years old (or to twenty-four years old if one includes graduate study) taking place on campus, by means of traditional methods of teaching and learning. It is true that extension courses, often on a noncredit basis, were made available to adults by some institutions, but this was a peripheral activity at best and generally had low status within the academic community. There has, however, in the past few years been a virtual revolution in American thought on the question of how, and for whom, higher education should be made available. This revolution is generally known by the somewhat awkward name "nontraditional higher education." It is of course by no means a uniquely American phenomenon, and it is well advanced in several other countries.

The revolution is taking place along two dimensions: "delivery systems" and "clientele," to use some ugly jargon. Under the former, there has been a proliferation of new—at least new here—techniques. These include external degrees, credit by examination, credit for experience gained outside higher education, and credit for training in industry. In addition, one now finds individualized, self-paced learning, and a wide expansion of two older ideas, the interweaving of higher education and employment and part-time study for degrees.

Under the dimension of new clientele, the new delivery systems have made it possible for higher education to reach out effectively to groups of people it did not previously serve or serve well. For example, higher education is now available to employed adults seeking improved qualifications or a career change, housewives seeking to enter or reenter the labor market after raising their children, members of the armed forces preparing to reenter civilian life, handicapped people of all ages, adults seeking a renewal of spirit and enrichment of their lives for its own sake, and people who missed their chance to go to college earlier in life because of discrimination, financial hardship, family responsibilities, or personal choice.

One must not overstate the importance of the nontraditional higher education movement. There is always the chance that it may turn out to have been a transitory fad. My own view, however, is that this is one of a small number of permanent innovations in the history of American higher education, ranking in importance with the land grant colleges movement, the introduction of graduate education from Germany in the latter half of the nineteenth century, and the emergence of the junior or community college in this century.

Lifelong learning will not involve everyone. The majority of adults will not want to put in the sustained effort required. Nonetheless, it will, I believe, interest enough adults to stimulate a large new demand for higher education, offered in ways and at times adults can manage. Already there are 3.6 million people past the age of twenty-four enrolled in our colleges and universities—over one-third of the total enrollment. In the coming decade, the expected increase in the twenty-four to forty-four year old population group will probably push the enrollment of older persons higher yet, both in absolute numbers and on a percentage basis.

In time, the introduction of new kinds of flexibility, on behalf of adults, into tradition-bound academic institutions is likely to have a considerable effect both on the way the institutions are organized and on their teaching methods for conventional students. It should also, in due course, begin to affect favorably the general public's attitude toward higher education. In New York State, which has pioneered in nontraditional programs, there is already evidence of impressive legislative support for the new approach, which is indicative of public approval.

There is, it is true, some concern being expressed about the quality of the degrees being granted in these new, unconventional ways. Proponents of the movement, however, are generally well aware of the danger of shoddy standards and are taking great care to make the new degree programs as rigorous as conventionally granted degrees and, in some cases, even more rigorous.

6
The Needs of Youth

It is illuminating to look at the issue of access within the broader social context of the needs of American youth generally. There are many reasons why young people attend college here. Some have a genuine interest in learning for its own sake. Some wish to prepare themselves for the professions or for other occupations. Some are seeking a maturing social experience away from home. Some see higher education as their only hope of raising their social and economic status above that of their parents. Some are simply seeking the credential (of a degree) for whatever it may be worth. Some are interested in improving their marriage prospects. And finally, some have no particular reason for going to college other than lack of anything else to occupy their time.

Thus, higher education means different things to different people, but for certain young people—perhaps quite a few—it simply represents a safe holding-pattern until they are old enough to land on adult ground. This may seem an expensive way for a society to induct its youth into adulthood. In our cost-sharing system, however, in which overall nearly half the cost is a private burden, higher education is considerably less expensive than other institutional arrangements for youth, such as military service, civilian service programs, prison, hospitalization for drug addiction, and so on, where the entire cost is a public burden. Furthermore, by providing young people with something at least moderately constructive to do, higher education may prevent antisocial activities which would ultimately cost the nation much more. Therefore, despite the burden the reluctant student places on higher education, from society's standpoint, until there is a good alternative, the presence of youth in higher education can be regarded as being in the public interest.

Some might argue that young people such as these should probably be working and not swelling the numbers in our colleges and universities. That argument, however, presumes the availability of jobs for youth. In fact, youth unemployment is very high at the present time, about 20 percent overall, better than 40 percent for young minority group males generally, and over 60 percent for sixteen-year old black male high school dropouts. This problem may be alleviated somewhat if the economy continues to improve. Indeed, there are those who believe there will be an abundance of jobs for youth by the 1980s because the population of the youth cohort will decline by then.

It is more likely in my view, that we are facing a long-term structural problem of youth unemployment, caused by a number of factors including the large-scale entry of adult women into the labor force in recent years. Some thirty-seven million women are now employed (or actively seeking employment) constituting 40 percent of the total U.S. labor force of about ninety-four million people. The labor force, in turn, comprises over 43 percent of the total population, a high proportion by previous American standards or by world standards, although not as high as in Japan or Sweden. The question in this country is whether a fully functioning economy *can* produce enough jobs for everyone who needs to or wants to work. If it cannot, young people will be the first to be left out, because they are less skilled, because they are considered to be less responsible employees than adults, and because it is the prevailing and understandable view of our trade unions that, in a shortage of jobs, preference should go to adults.

A fundamental issue in American life today, therefore, is whether the nation does not need, for the first time in its history, to formulate a coherent set of policies for its youth—a program that would include youth service projects, the creation of employment opportunities, the integration of education and employment, and traditional higher education. If such a coherent set of policies were worked out and implemented, the impact on higher education could be considerable.

On the one hand, such policies might largely remove the reluctant students, the young person who is in college *faute de mieux,* and allow institutions to concentrate their efforts on the more highly motivated students. On the other hand, it could serve to stimulate colleges and universities to develop, in conjunction with employers, new programs of combined study and work that would appeal to youngsters who are bored or disillusioned with traditional education. Following such a course would, naturally, imply spending less money on higher education for the young and devoting funds to other activities for them. It would not, however, necessarily mean a decline in the total demand for higher education, because, as I have suggested earlier, increased enrollment by adults would probably be taking up the slack. Nevertheless, it would probably mean that some nonselective, private, liberal arts colleges offering traditional academic programs to college-age youth would lose enough of their present clientele to be forced to close. While that would be unfortunate, it would not be a disaster for the nation.

The Preservation of "Elitism"

In the United States, as in many other nations, a wave of public skepticism toward higher education has developed in the past half dozen years. The new doubts seem to have been based on a variety of factors: a residue of public resentment over campus unrest in the sixties; reaction to an oversell of the pecuniary advantages of obtaining a degree; disillusionment with the university's capacity to help solve great social problems in the face of earlier inflated claims to that effect; the growing cost of higher education to the taxpayer, to students, and to their families; economic recession, which has caused a seeming oversupply of graduates; and other elements.

In most of the states, this new skepticism has resulted in a diminished level of general support for higher education, relative to the rising cost of operating institutions due to inflation and to ever-increasing enrollments. Federal support of research at the universities has also declined markedly in relation to rising costs during this period.

In addition, at the state level the past decade has seen a widespread resurgence of the kinds of egalitarianism and parochialism that have ebbed and flowed in American life throughout the nation's history. Under the former, there has been an effort in some states, often politically inspired, to build up smaller, regionally oriented public institutions at the expense of the—allegedly elitist—distinguished state universities. Under the latter, the effort has been to diminish the national, in some cases international, role of the leading state universities, on the grounds that they should be serving purely state needs.

In short, the past few years have been ones in which powerful economic, social, and political forces have operated to restrict further progress of some of our greatest public universities as institutions of acknowledged world standard in advanced research and postgraduate training.

This is a serious matter in itself, but has been made doubly unfortunate by the severe problems concurrently faced by our great private universities because of inflation and economic recession.

Without exception, these institutions have found it virtually impossible to control escalating costs for personnel, student assistance, security, energy and fuel, library acquisition, maintainence, and so on. Income, it is true, has also risen, as the result of increases in tuitions and more generous private donations by alumni and others. But no sooner have budgets been brought into balance through vigorous, heroic cost-cutting efforts than new projections have revealed further deficits ahead. At the same time, the reduction of federal support for research and graduate training has hit private universities particularly hard.

In these circumstances, those who are responsible for managing the leading public and private universities, particularly their presidents, have become seriously concerned about the future of the highest level of intellectual effort in this country. They are troubled about the adequacy of support for basic research, for research libraries, and for graduate fellowships. A special worry is the field of international studies, in which some important areas and language programs that must certainly be regarded as national resources have already had to be discontinued or cut so deeply their effectiveness has been impaired.

A group of leading university presidents is therefore working together actively to find new ways of making the case for their institutions to the nation's political leadership. This would seem a straightforward enough task, but in fact, is fraught with difficulties. In the first place, in the aftermath of what many politicians would regard as overly lavish support of universities during the decade of the sixties and early into the seventies, it has the appearance of self-interested pleading and an unwillingness to make the kinds of patriotic sacrifices demanded by less affluent times and competing public needs. Secondly, in an age when egalitarianism is perhaps more ascendant in American life than it has been since the Jacksonian era of the 1840s, the defense of universities—which by their very nature must be highly selective in their functioning—can be portrayed by those who do not understand such institutions, or have suppressed resentment of them, as undemocratic and elitist. Thirdly, many of the rationales used in earlier eras for development of the nation's research capacity are no longer in favor with significant sectors of the public. For example, the argument that advanced research is essential to the nation's defense runs into strong post-Vietnam feelings that universities should keep clear of anything to do with the military—even though research and how it is used are obviously two very different things.

Again, the argument that international studies programs at universities are essential to the nation's future performance in foreign affairs encounters resurgent isolationism, growing antipathy to Third World nations, and mounting disenchantment with the United Nations—however dismaying such sentiments are to many Americans.

Finally, the argument that high-level research and training in the universities are essential to the solution of major domestic problems and to the general social and economic progress of the nation runs into widespread skepticism today. It even encounters in some groups, especially among some young people, an antagonism, based on moral grounds, to the very idea of "progress."

In theory, it should not have to fall to university presidents to make the public case for our most highly distinguished educational institutions. Certainly, it should not fall on them alone. Many other voices should be heard—in legislative bodies, among appointed officials, in industry and labor, in the media, in the professions, and elsewhere. But, in fact, because of the kinds of social currents I have described, these voices simply are not being heard at the moment. The kind of "elitism" in higher education that is necessary to keep the nation's stock of high-level intellectual capital replenished must, therefore, ironically be defended by the very people who in these egalitarian times are probably the most handicapped for the task.

Institutional Autonomy

Recent years have unquestionably seen a marked restriction of the autonomy of many individual colleges and universities in this country. The reasons for this are varied. I shall touch on just three.

First, as higher education expanded rapidly in the decade of the sixties in response to insistent public demand, its political attractiveness to elected officials in the fifty states rose accordingly, from a relatively low level to considerable heights. In 1960, state expenditure on higher education averaged about 0.4 percent of personal income. By 1975, fifteen years later, it had become 1.09 percent, a figure which represented about 15 percent of annual state budgets. In that same period the number of students for whom the states, joined in some cases by local authorities, were providing places in public institutions rose from 2.1 million to 7.8 million, while the number of public institutions rose from 750 to 1,452. It was inevitable, in these circumstances, that politicians would take a direct, personal interest in higher education and through inexperience, or because they sensed a new area for political advantage, begin to interfere in the internal affairs of particular institutions.

Later, after about 1970, as public opinion gradually began to cool toward higher education, politicians sensed a different kind of political advantage in adding to, and even leading, the mounting chorus of attacks on it. In some states they became actively hostile to higher education and sought, through restrictive legislation, to abridge the traditional freedoms enjoyed by academic institutions.

It would be wrong, however, to represent the political interest in higher education as having been entirely cynically motivated. The vast expansion of public higher education and, in recent years, growing state aid to private institutions, did present elected officials with genuine problems of how higher education should best be organized and governed to meet a broad public interest, and how it could be made reasonably accountable to the taxpayer for the huge sums of money being spent on it.

It would be impossible here to try to describe the varied and complex ways in which the states have gone about solving this tripartite problem of organization, governance, and accountability. It is sufficient to say that in virtually every state some new piece of governmental or quasigovernmental machinery, standing between academic institutions on the one hand and the state government on the other, has been created. Some of these new bodies are purely voluntary coordinating and planning agencies. Others have compulsory coordinating powers, and some are actual governing boards overseeing the management of large numbers of institutions.

Inevitably, these new agencies, manned by their own professional staffs, have taken over much of the authority and responsibility formerly vested in the boards of individual institutions. Unfortunate as this is, the alternative in many states would have been duplication, waste, lack of planning to meet total state needs, and political rivalry between institutions in state legislatures. Not that these problems have been totally eliminated by the new coordinating and governing machinery, but they have certainly been alleviated in most states through this means.[2]

A second major force impinging on institutional autonomy in recent years has been the federal government. It is not that Washington has sought to interfere directly in the management of individual institutions for specific educational reasons. It is rather that federal officials in carrying out the requirements of about a dozen major pieces of legislation dealing with other matters—such as racial and sexual discrimination, environmental protection, family rights and privacy, occupational safety and health, and so on—have been obliged to impose new regulations. In general, it has been the fact of federal financial assistance to academic institutions that has given the federal government its right to interfere. Quite recently, however, at least one federal agency has been taking the position that the receipt of scholarship aid by students gives it the necessary standing to regulate the institutions attended by such students. This issue has yet to be fought out in the courts.

While federal laws and Supreme Court interpretations of the Constitution now impinge on higher education in a wide variety of ways, it is in the equal opportunity area that the sharpest controversy has arisen. In this area the federal government has the authority not only to prevent institutions from discriminating against minorities and women in all aspects of their operations but also, as I have mentioned earlier, to draw up and obtain federal approval of affirmative action plans to rectify present imbalances caused by past discrimination. Unfortunately, the federal administration of its affirmative action responsibilities has been so clumsy, inefficient, and at times seemingly vindicative in spirit, that it has aroused widespread antagonism in the higher education community, even among some administrators with a strong commitment to equal opportunity.

Beyond those who believe in affirmative action but consider federal administration of it to be now quite thoroughly discredited, there are others in the academic community who believe that the very idea of affirmative action is a violation of academic freedom. They say it imposes external considerations on the manner in which the faculty exercises its traditional right to decide who shall be hired to teach and who promoted to tenured rank.

On the other side of the issue, organizations concerned with the rights of minorities and women, far from considering federal administration of affirmative action too onerous, believe it has been too slow and ineffectual. It is the view of these organizations that the academic community, dominated as it is by white males, will never give minorities and women a really equal chance unless pressure is applied. They too recognize the need for improved federal procedures, but they are fearful, nonetheless, that any administrative changes might weaken the federal role. Thus, while no one is particularly happy about affirmative action, it will probably, because of the balance of forces for and against it, continue pretty much as it is for a considerable time to come.

A third force impinging on institutional autonomy is the relatively new phenomenon of faculty unionization. Three organizations—the National Education Association, the American Federation of Teachers, and the American Association of University Professors—are currently competing with each other to become bargaining agents for faculty, either in specific institutions or in entire state systems of higher education. They represent the faculties on matters relating to salaries, benefits, and conditions of employment. Only about 15 percent of faculty members are currently unionized, but unionization is gradually spreading and seems likely to continue to do so. Before an election to determine whether a union is to be recognized can take place on the campus of a public institution, a state must pass legislation which legalizes collective bargaining by public employees. About half of the states now have such laws on their books. Among public systems of higher education those of New York, New Jersey, and Hawaii are now fully unionized. Collective bargaining in private institutions, however, is not regulated by state law. It is subject, rather, to federal regulation by the National Labor Relations Board.

The experience with unionization has been somewhat mixed. At some institutions it has aroused distrust between pro- and anti-union faculty members and between faculty and administration. In such instances it has contributed to a poisoning of the atmosphere that is harmful to everyone and especially the students. In other institutions, it has materially improved the status of the faculty without damaging internal relationships or affecting the interests of students adversely.

In general, the very idea of unionization appears contrary to the traditional American concept of academic self-government by collegial consensus, wherein the faculty, administration, and board of trustees each has its respective rights and responsibilities, which together make-up a collective concern for the welfare of the institution. Now, a new element of authority has intruded — the legally binding union contract, derived from an adversarial relationship between administrations and governing boards (now defined as employers) on the one hand, and faculty members (now defined as employees) on the other. In the process of collective bargaining, demands are likely to be made on behalf of "employees" which the "employer" does not have the power to agree to, because honoring them requires appropriations of funds or other actions by state officials. Therefore, the real bargaining agent on management's side becomes the governor or legislature, or both. On labor's side, since the faculty at large cannot possibly participate in the complex negotiating process, responsibility must be delegated to elected or appointed representatives, in effect union officials.

In the end, the nature if instituional governance has been profoundly altered: authority has moved outside the institution to public officials, and it has moved outside the faculty *per se* to professional union officials. In the process, institutional autonomy has virtually disappeared in some very important areas.

In fairness, it must be recognized that the traditional concept of consensus governance, based on shared power and responsibility, was always a myth in some institutions where faculty were in fact treated as little more than hired hands and regarded themselves as such. In such cases, unionization can hardly be regarded as contributing to a loss of institutional autonomy through vitiation of the faculty role in governance. Indeed, it may, for the first time, have given the faculty at least some voice in decisions that greatly affect their welfare.

These, then, are three of the forces that are acting to undermine the autonomy of individual colleges and universities today. They are forces which tend to affect public institutions more heavily than private: although, as the latter steadily become more dependent on public support for their survival, their independence is also threatened.

Institutional autonomy is, of course, not such a self-evident good that it can be defended blindly. Having it does not automatically guarantee high standards of academic performance and integrity; lack of it does not always result in a poor institution. Autonomy can indeed serve as a cloak for sloth, undeserved privilege, and unjustified resistance to change on the part of both faculty and administration.

Nor is it self-evident that government is always malevolent. In the United States, it is fashionable these days to berate so-called big government, especially big government in Washington. Some of this rhetoric is no doubt justified, but much of it reflects pure fantasy and a kind of national self-delusion. Big government is not something that has been visited on us by evil beings from another planet or by allegedly mindless or malicious bureaucrats. It is no more than the conscientious efforts of generally well-motivated fellow Americans to give effect to laws passed by democratically elected legislative bodies, presumably expressing the popular will. Some of the alarm over government interference in institutions has, it seems to me, lacked that sense of perspective.

Nonetheless, all things considered, institutional autonomy is important to the overall quality of a nation's higher educational effort. Academic institutions, by their very nature, do tend to perform best if given as much freedom as possible by the societies they serve. This is particularly true in regard to research, where too much bureaucratic interference and a denial of government support for basic enquiry in favor of narrowly specified, mission-oriented investigation can result in poor quality, pedestrian work, the stultifying of fundamental scientific advance, and much waste.

Autonomy is also crucial in regard to the university's performance of its traditional role of dispassionate, objective, social critic. Although academics have sometimes abused their positions of sanctuary, when they have used it rightly and conscientiously to provide disinterested, expert opinion in their paticular fields of competence, they have provided society with an invaluable service it simply cannot afford to do without.

I do not believe we have yet reached a point in this country where the right of academic institutions to carry out basic research in an unfettered manner and to serve as objective social critic is under *general* and *direct* attack. I do believe, however, that further erosion of autonomy could gradually create an atmosphere which is inimicable to the highest level and quality of research and social analysis in our institutions. We should, therefore, be concerned over the decline of institutional autonomy and should seek to prevent its further erosion. In my opinion, this can best be accomplished not by sweeping public attacks on governmental bureaucracy but by patient, quiet discussion between representatives of the academic world and appropriate elected and appointed officials. If and when that fails, but only then, other approaches would be both necessary and justified.

Some Final Thoughts

Discussion of these four topics—access, the needs of youth, elitism, and autonomy—has, I hope, indicated that here in the United States we simultaneously attach value to two quite different concepts of higher education. According to the first, we view higher education essentially as a social service, an activity that should be pragmatically and fluidly related to the ever-changing needs of the society, available to all and closely responsive to the popular will. According to the second, we view it as something that should be independent of society, self-directed, slow to respond to the fashions and currents of the day, housed in a set of unique, selective institutions whose sole purpose is to foster the highest levels of intellectual development and achievement.

These two concepts are inherently contradictory and are bound to produce constant tension, not only within the total system of higher education but often within individual institutions. Their existence goes far to explain the apparent confusion of purpose which foreign critics, and indeed many Americans, see as a basic weakness in higher education here. This duality of approach, however, also produces much of the special strength of American higher education, because the constant play of one concept on the other—the rivalry between them—makes for a system that is both dynamic and conservative, responsive to society and aloof from it, hospitable to change and slow to abandon traditional values, pliable and inflexible, democratic and elitist, nonselective and selective.

Whatever its strengths and weaknesses, higher education in the United States is uniquely American in its nature and cannot properly be understood or judged outside its American context. Because of this uniqueness, I have never believed that comprehensive guidelines for the development of higher education in the new nations of the Commonwealth are to be found here, or that Americans should preach the superiority of their system at large or try to be missionaries for any particular aspect of it.

What American higher education does constitute is an immense resource — extensive, rich in the variety and profusion of its expression, open to all comers. In an enterprise of such magnitude there is certain to be some experience that can be of value to others, and particularly to the leaders of higher education in new nations.

FOOTNOTES

1. Since this statement was presented, a case of major proportions has emerged and is now before the Supreme Court. It is the case of Allan Bakke who charges the University of California (Medical School at Davis) with "reverse discrimination." Mr. Bakke claims that "race-conscious" admissions practices give preference to minority students over his candidacy as a white. The judgment of the Court will have far-reaching social and political as well as educational effects.
2. If this subject interests the reader particularly, I would recommend a recent publication of The Carnegie Foundation for the Advancement of Teaching entitled, *The States and Higher Education*.

DESIGN AND FUNCTION

John R. Shea

Institutions and Enrollments

According to the *Education Directory of Colleges and Universities, 1975-76,* there were approximately 2,800 institutions of higher education in the United States in 1975-76.[1] The exact number depends on whether branches of multicampus universities are counted as separate institutions. If they are, the total is 3,026.[2] The two most populous states—New York and California—ranked first and second with 285 and 247 campuses. Wyoming and Nevada, two sparsely populated states, had only eight and six campuses, respectively.

Of the 3,026 campuses, those which are major institutions that award doctoral degrees number less than 200—yet they enrolled over one-fourth of the over eleven million students at the opening of the Fall 1975 term (see Table 1).[3] Nearly 500 campuses are classified as comprehensive colleges and universities with one or more professional or occupational programs in addition to the liberal arts. Many institutions in this category were formerly teachers colleges, but have now extended their program offerings to include the liberal arts. Others are traditional liberal arts colleges which have added programs in such areas as business administration, nursing or engineering. Comprehensive colleges and universities enrolled nearly three million students (26 percent of the total) in Fall 1975. Liberal arts colleges are numerous—there are 724—but typically small in enrollment. Larger liberal arts colleges often resemble more comprehensive institutions, and the distinction between the two necessarily involves judgment. As a group, liberal arts colleges while accounting for nearly one-quarter of all campuses, enrolled only 7 percent of all students. Two-year

TABLE 1
Number of Institutions of Higher Education and Enrollment, by Carnegie Classification, Fall 1975

	Number	Institutions[1] Percent	Public	Private	Public as % of Total
Total	3,026	100.0	1,442	1,584	47.7
Doctoral-Granting	173	5.7	109	64	63.0
Research Univ I	52	1.7	30	22	57.7
Research Univ II	39	1.3	27	12	69.2
Other, I, II	82	2.7	52	30	63.4
Comprehensive Universities and Colleges	476	15.7	332	144	69.7
Liberal Arts Colleges	724	23.9	26	698	3.6
Liberal Arts I	139	4.6	2	137	1.4
Liberal Arts II	585	19.3	24	561	4.1
Two-Year Institutions	1,128	37.3	897	231	79.5
Specialized Institutions	525	17.3	78	447	14.9
	Enrollment (in number of thousands)[1]			
Total	11,148[2]	100.0	8,798	2,350	78.9
Doctoral-Granting	3,007	27.0	2,338	669	77.7
Research Univ I	1,226	11.0	965	260	78.8
Research Univ II	695	6.2	579	115	83.4
Other I, II	1,087	9.7	793	294	73.0
Comprehensive Universities and Colleges	2,938	26.4	2,388	550	81.3
Liberal Arts Colleges	765	6.9	63	702	8.2
Liberal Arts I	205	1.8	14	190	7.1
Liberal Arts II	560	5.0	48	511	8.7
Two-Year Institutions	3,974	35.6	3,824	150	96.2
Specialized Institutions	464	4.2	186	278	40.1

Source: Unpublished tabulations from Higher Education General Information Survey.
[1] Both number and percent may not add to total because of rounding.
[2] Preliminary enrollment figures; thus, number differs slightly from total shown in Table 2.

institutions—for the most part junior or community colleges—represent over one-third of the total number of colleges, universities, and branch campuses, and account for nearly the same fraction of total enrollment. The term "specialized institution" is used to encompass a variety of special-purpose institutions, such as

TABLE 2

Selected Characteristics of Institutions of Higher Education, by Control, 1975-76 (percentage distribution)[1]

	Total	Public	Private
Number of Campuses	3,026	1,442	1,584
Main Campus or Branch			
Main Campus	91.4	84.5	97.6
Branch	8.6	15.5	2.4
University	0.1	0.2	—
Other 4-year	4.3	6.7	2.1
2-year	4.3	8.7	0.3
Highest Level of Offering			
Doctorate	13.3	13.5	13.0
Graduate Nondegree Granting and Beyond Master's But Less than Doctorate	5.4	6.0	4.8
Master's or First-Professional Degree	18.4	11.8	24.3
4- or 5-Year Baccalaureate Degree[2]	25.7	6.4	43.3
2 But Less than 4 Years Beyond High School	37.3	62.2	14.6
Race of Students			
Historically Black Colleges	3.3	2.9	3.7
Other	96.7	97.3	96.3
Sex of Students			
Coedicational[3]	91.8	99.4	85.0
Men Only	3.9	0.5[4]	7.1
Women Only	4.3	0.1	8.0

Source: U.S. National Center for Education Statistics (1977a), pp. 104-108; and Blake, Lambert, and Martin (1974), pp. A-1 to A-6.

[1] Detail may not add to 100.0 because of rounding.

[2] Includes fifteen private undergraduate nondegree granting institutions.

[3] Includes twelve private institutions with separate colleges for men and for women.

[4] In Fall 1976, the four U.S. service academies admitted women for the first time.

seminaries, bible colleges, separate medical and other health professional schools, and schools of business administration, engineering, law, art, and music. Many of these specialized campuses are small. In total, they enrolled only 4 percent of all students in Fall 1975.

Table 2 presents other characteristics regarding the 3,026 colleges, universities, and branch campuses, which comprise the universe of higher education in the United States. Over 250 are branches of multicampus institutions, and about half of these are two-year campuses.[4] Approximately 100 are institutions initially established to serve blacks. Although the trend in the last decade has been toward coeducation, nearly 250 colleges still serve either men or women but not both.

As already suggested, colleges and universities vary enormously in enrollment size. In 1975, public institutions enrolled, on the average, just over 6,100 students per campus, compared to 1,500 per private institution. The extent of variation on these mean values can be seen in Figure 1. The diagonal line indicates what the relationship between number of institutions and their cumulative enrollment would be if each public or private institution had the same number of students. For example, 60 percent of the institutions would account for 60 percent of total enrollment. In reality, a large number of small institutions account for a small proportion of total enrollments, while a small number of large institutions account for a large proportion. For example, about 1,200 campuses (40 percent of the total), each enrolling less than 1,000 students, accounted for only 5 percent of total enrollment in Fall 1975. At the other extreme, twenty-seven campuses (less than 1 percent) each with 30,000 or more students, enrolled nearly 10 percent of the total.[5]

Approximately half of all colleges and universities are controlled by public authorities. Of the remainder (1,584 campuses), about half or 802 are organized as independent nonprofit institutions; the rest are associated with a religious organization or church.[6] Among institutions in the public sector, nearly three-fifths are state institutions, organized under the constitution or statutes of each state (see Figure 2). These 836 campuses comprise the major state universities, including the nation's land grant institutions, as well as many state colleges, which now typically offer an array of programs at the baccalaureate and master's degree levels. Public institutions controlled at the local level, or which are governed by state and local authorities, include a few four-year institutions but, in the main, are campuses with two-year programs (junior or community colleges) leading to the associate degree. There are nine federally controlled institutions; these comprise the eight United States Service Schools (for example, West Point) and Haskell Indian Junior College.

Both the number of institutions of higher education and total enrollments have risen dramatically over the last two decades (Figure 3). Between 1955 and 1975, for example, the number of

FIGURE 1

Percentage of Institutions of Higher Education and Branches, by Control, and Their Percentage of Enrollment in Control Category, Fall 1975

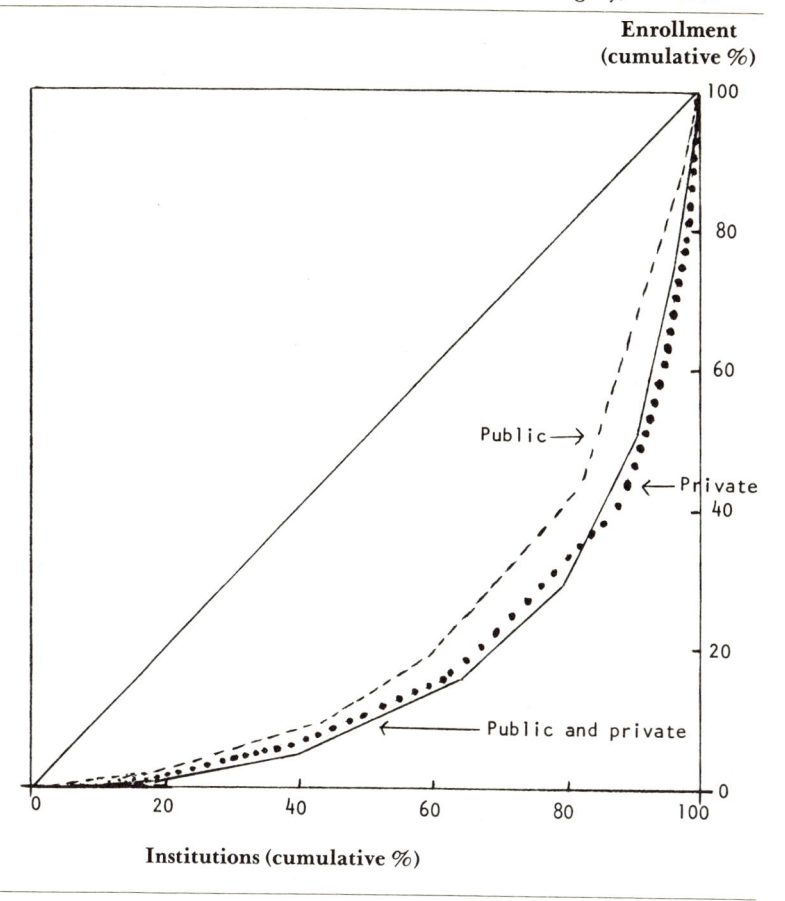

Source: U.S. National Center for Education Statistics (1977a), p. 105.
Note:

Calculated from grouped data	Institution	Enrollment (Degree & Nondegree)
Public	1,442	8,834,508
Private	1,584	2,350,351
Public and private	3,026	11,184,859

FIGURE 2

Colleges, Universities, and Branch Campuses, by Control: Number and Percent of Total Public or Total Private, 1975-76

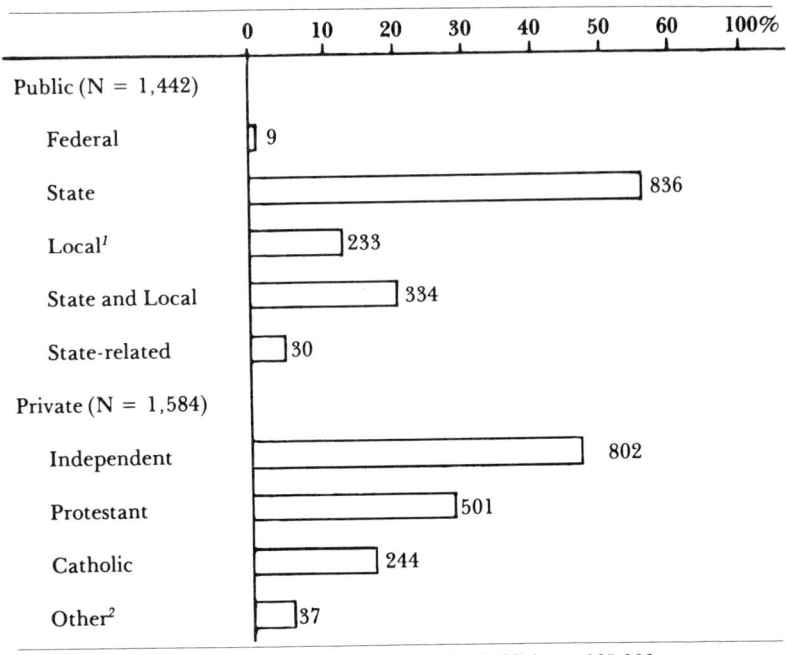

	Number
Public (N = 1,442)	
Federal	9
State	836
Local[1]	233
State and Local	334
State-related	30
Private (N = 1,584)	
Independent	802
Protestant	501
Catholic	244
Other[2]	37

Source: U.S. National Center for Education Statistics (1977a), pp. 105-106.

[1] City, county, or district.
[2] Includes Jewish, Latter Day Saints, Greek Orthodox, Russian Orthodox, and Unitarian.

institutions (not counting the branches of multicampus institutions) jumped by 50 percent—from 1,849 to 2,765—with the number of two-year colleges clearly outpacing expansion in four-year institutions. Total degree-credit enrollment increased much faster, rising over the twenty-year period from 2.7 million to 9.7 million, or over three-and-one-half times. Nondegree credit enrollment, which includes students in occupational or general studies programs not chiefly creditable towards a bachelor's degree, rose at an even faster clip—from 151,00 in 1955 to 1,453,000 in 1975.[7] Enrollment expanded in both public and private institutions, but the proportion of public colleges and universities rose from 56 percent of the total in 1955 to 76 percent in 1975. The fastest growing type of institution has been the two-year college. Even excluding nondegree-credit enrollments, public two-year institutions, which enrolled 10 percent of the 2.7 million degree-credit students of 1955, accounted for one-quarter of the 9.7 million in 1975.

FIGURE 3

Percentage of Institutions of Higher Education and of Degree-credit Enrollment, by Level and Control, Fall 1955 and 1975

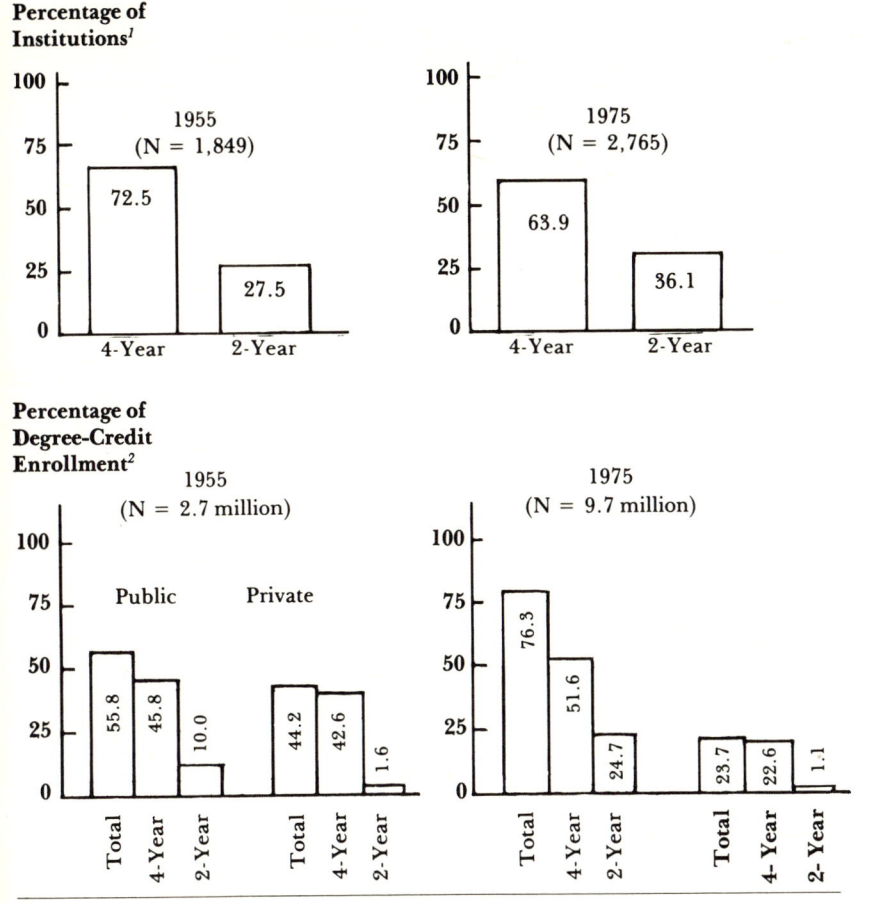

Percentage of Institutions[1]

1955 (N = 1,849): 4-Year 72.5; 2-Year 27.5

1975 (N = 2,765): 4-Year 63.9; 2-Year 36.1

Percentage of Degree-Credit Enrollment[2]

1955 (N = 2.7 million):
- Public: Total 55.8; 4-Year 45.8; 2-Year 10.0
- Private: Total 44.2; 4-Year 42.6; 2-Year 1.6

1975 (N = 9.7 million):
- Public: Total 76.3; 4-Year 51.6; 2-Year 24.7
- Private: Total 23.7; 4-Year 22.6; 2-Year 1.1

Source: U.S. National Center for Educational Statistics (1966), pp. 11-12; and (1977a), pp. 87, 104.

[1] Branches *not* counted separately.
[2] Students enrolled in branch campuses are counted in category of parent institution.

Table 3 presents selected characteristics of the 11,185,000 students enrolled in Fall 1975, along with their full-time equivalent number. Of the 11.2 million students, 55 percent were men, 61 percent attended full-time, and 64 percent were enrolled in undergraduate degree-credit programs. Full-time equivalent enrollment amounted to 8,481,000, nondegree-credit students representing 12 percent of this total.

TABLE 3
Enrollment in Institutions of Higher Education, by Selected Characteristics, Fall 1975

	Number (in thousands)[1]	Percent[1]
Total (headcount)	11,185	100
Public	8,835	79
Private	2,350	21
Men	6,149	55
Women	5,036	45
Full-Time	6,841	61
Part-Time	4,344	39
Degree-Credit	9,731	87
Undergraduate	7,179	64
First professional	242	2
Graduate	1,263	11
Unclassified	1,047	9
First-time	1,910	17
Continuing	7,821	70
Nondegree-Credit	1,453	13
4-Year Institutions	7,314	65
2-Year Institutions	3,871	35
Total (full-time equivalent)	8,481	100
Public	6,523	77
Private	1,958	23
Full-Time	6,841	81
Part-Time	1,640	19
Degree-Credit	7,495	88
Nondegree-Credit	986	12

Source: U.S. National Center for Education Statistics (1977a), pp. 80-81; and (1976b), pp. 16, 20.

[1] May not add to total because of rounding.

A questionnaire survey of 25,000 undergraduates, conducted in 1975 by the Carnegie Council on Policy Studies in Higher Education, revealed that three in seven students reside in college dormitories or in other college housing (Table 4). Another 2 percent live in fraternity or sorority houses. Living on-campus is the typical pattern for liberal arts colleges, many of which are located in small towns. Doctoral-granting and comprehensive institutions, which vary in location, are typically large and serve students from both

TABLE 4

Housing Arrangements of Undergraduate Students, by Carnegie Classification of Institutions, 1975[1]

Percent[2]

Carnegie Classification	Total Percent	College Dorm or Other College Housing	Fraternity or Sorority House	House of Parent or Other Relative	Other[3]
Doctoral-Granting	100%	39	6	14	41
Comprehensive Universities and Colleges	100	36	1	30	33
Liberal Arts Colleges	100	62	2	15	21
Two-Year Institutions	100	8	—[5]	41	51
Total (average)[4]	100	30	2	28	40

Source: 1975 Carnegie Council Undergraduate Survey.

[1] The survey question addressed to the students was: "Where did you live most of the time during your most recent college term?"

[2] Detail may not add to 100.0 because of rounding.

[3] Includes rooming house, rented room, apartment or house (not parents'), and other (unspecified).

[4] Weighted average, including specialized institutions not shown separately.

[5] Less than 0.5 percent.

urban and rural areas—including large numbers of out-of-state students. These institutions have the most "balanced" living arrangements. About two-fifths lives on, or near, the campus in sponsored housing. One one-third live in rented or other quarters (not their parents'). One in five live at home with adult relatives. Two in five students attending two-year colleges lives with their parents; over half live in their own houses, apartments, or rooms. Over two-thirds of all United States undergraduates live off-campus. Some live close by; others commute daily to and from school.

Although *not* a part of higher education, as that term is used in the United States, over 8,000 noncollegiate schools offer occupational programs for postsecondary youth and adults (Table 5).[8] Nearly 1,000 are public institutions, such as area vocational-technical institutes, many of which have been established since passage of the Vocational Education Act of 1963. Others are private specialty schools, generally proprietary in form, offering one or a

TABLE 5

Number and Enrollment of Noncollegiate Postsecondary Schools with Occupational Programs by Type and Control, 1975-76[1]

Type of School	Institutions Total	Institutions Percent Public[2]	Enrollment[3] Number (in thousands)	Enrollment[3] Percent	Students per School
All Types (Total or Average)	8,356	11.5	1,733	100.0	207
Vocational-Technical	1,887	31.5	463	26.7	245
Technical Institute	210	18.1	91	5.3	433
Business/Office	1,140	0.1	326	18.8	286
Cosmetology/Barber	2,328	0.9	132	7.6	57
Flight	1,309	3.4	72	4.1	55
Trade	723	4.1	153	8.8	211
Correspondence	106	—	388	22.4	3,665
Hospital	1,112	19.3	71	4.1	64
Other	241	8.7	38	2.2	157

Source: U.S. National Center for Education Statistics (1977c), pp. 176, 180.

[1] Includes Puerto Rico in addition to the fifty states and Washington, D.C.
[2] Private includes proprietary schools (profit-seeking), independent (nonprofit) schools, and schools operated by religious groups.
[3] Detail may not add to total because of rounding.

TABLE 6

Estimated Expenditures for Higher Education, by Purpose and Control, 1975-76

	Total	Public	Private
	(in billions of current dollars)		
Total, Current and Capital	$44.8	$30.4	$14.4
Capital Outlay	5.1	3.6	1.5
Current Expenditures and Interest	39.7	26.8	12.9
Current Expenditures, by Purpose			
Educational and General	32.5	22.7	9.8
Student Education[1]	25.6	18.2	7.4
Research[2]	3.3	2.2	1.1
Scholarships and Fellowships[3]	1.8	0.9	0.9
Public Service[4]	1.8	1.4	0.4
Auxiliary Enterprises[5]	4.4	2.7	1.7
Hospitals and Independent Operations	3.8	2.1	1.7
Mandatory Transfers[6]	1.0	0.7	0.3

Source: U.S. National Center for Education Statistics (1977a), pp. 21-22; and (1976b), pp. 77-79; and Table 2.

[1] Instruction, academic support and student services, plant operation, and maintenance, and general institutional support.

[2] Sponsored or separately budgeted, except federally funded R&D centers, which are included with hospitals and other independent operations.

[3] Not considered an educational and general item prior to 1974-75; grants, stipends, and tuition or fee remissions.

[4] Cooperative extension and other, largely noninstructional services—primarily for groups external to the institution.

[5] Resident halls, food services, and the like.

[6] Debt service and similar required fund transfers.

few programs in specified areas such as commercial pilot training, barbering, or cosmetology. Yet others are nonprofit institutions, including a sizeable number of hospital schools of nursing, often associated with religious groups. During the 1975-76 school year, 1.7 million students were enrolled in noncollegiate postsecondary schools. The domain of adult education includes not only these students but well over ten milion others who take courses on a part-time basis from a variety of institutions—for example, colleges and universities, adult high schools, and community-based organizations such as the Red Cross. Estimates from the May 1975 Current Population Survey indicate the 17.1 million persons seventeen years old or over, who were not full-time students, took one or more courses in the twelve months preceding May 1975.[9] Aside from correspondence schools, the average length of each program was 1,100 hours, ranging from an average of 118 hours for commercial pilot training to 3,916 hours for those studying radiologic technology.[10]

Funding

It is estimated that in 1975, current and capital account expenditures for elementary, secondary, and higher education totaled $120 billion—7.9 percent of the Gross National Product.[11] Nearly $45 billion was expended by institutions of higher education for all purposes (Table 6). Of this amount, nearly $26 billion was allocated for instruction of students (including academic and student services) and general campus maintenance and support. Over $3 billion was expended on sponsored research. About $5.6 billion went toward public services of various kinds, including health care services of teaching hospitals and services of other independent operations.

Although not shown here, in 1975-76, full-time resident degree-credit students paid, on the average, $513 in public and $2333 in private institutions for tuition and required fees.[12]

Current fund expenditures for educational and general purposes by type of institution and control are shown in Table 7.[13] As one would expect, universities allocate considerably more resources to sponsored research than other institutions. Two-year colleges spend over 90 percent of their funds for student education.

In grant support, the federal government provides nearly $1 of every $6 spent by institutions of higher education (Figure 4).[14] Much of the money is for research and physical facilities. Nearly half the money expended by public institutions is derived from state and local taxes. The "other" category in Figure 4 includes student fees—part of which are ultimately paid from government sources—as well as receipts from auxiliary enterprises, private gifts and grants, nonfederal income from major public services, and other receipts. Direct federal and state aid to students has also increased dramatically. In 1970-71 "inclusive" aid to student programs, including loans and workstudy programs, totaled $2.2 billion; by 1974-75 federal and state student aid had increased to $3.5 billion.

Expenditures for Educational and General Purposes, by Type and Control, 1974-75[1]
(in millions of current dollars)

	Total	Student Education[2]	Research[3]	Scholarships and Fellowships[4]	Public Service[5]
Total Public	$18,889	$15,143	$2,071	$740	$935
Universities	7,902	5,450	1,480	334	639
Other 4-year	7,153	6,085	562	287	218
2-Year	3,835	3,608	29	118	79
Total Private	8,350	6,351	1,090	734	174
Universities	3,919	2,643	895	313	69
Other 4-Year	4,198	3,497	194	404	103
2-Year	233	212	1	17	2
			Percent[6]		
Average Total Public	100.0	80.2	11.0	3.9	5.0
Universities	100.0	69.0	18.7	4.2	8.1
Other 4-Year	100.0	85.1	7.9	4.0	3.0
2-Year	100.0	94.1	0.8	3.1	2.1
Average Total Private	100.0	76.1	13.1	8.8	2.1
Universities	100.0	67.4	22.8	8.0	1.8
Other 4-year	100.0	83.3	4.6	9.6	2.5
2-Year	100.0	91.1	0.5	7.4	1.0

Source: U.S. National Center for Education Statistics (1977d), pp. 4-5.
[1] Includes Puerto Rico and other outlying areas; may not add to total due to rounding.
[2] Instruction, academic support and student services, plan operation and maintenance, and general institutional support.
[3] Sponsored or separately budgeted; excludes federally funded R&D centers, which are not included as an "educational or general" purpose.
[4] Not considered an educational and general item prior to 1974-75; grants, stipends, and tuition or fee remissions.
[5] Cooperative extension and other, largely noninstructional services – primarily for groups external to the institution.
[6] May not add to 100.0 due to rounding.

FIGURE 4

Estimated Expenditures for Higher Education, Both Current and Capital Outlay, by Source of Funds and Control, 1975-76[1]

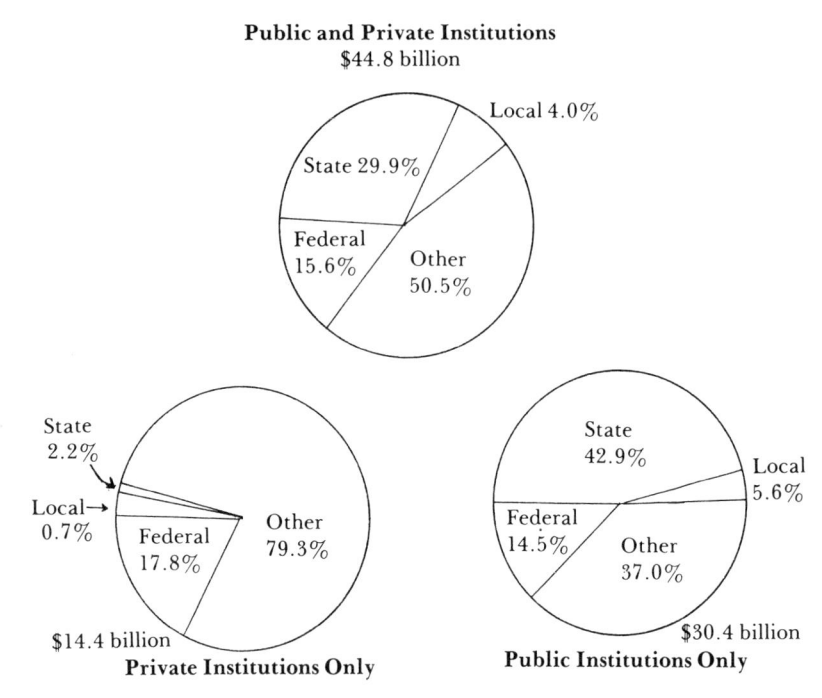

Public and Private Institutions
$44.8 billion

- State 29.9%
- Local 4.0%
- Federal 15.6%
- Other 50.5%

Private Institutions Only
$14.4 billion

- State 2.2%
- Local 0.7%
- Federal 17.8%
- Other 79.3%

Public Institutions Only
$30.4 billion

- State 42.9%
- Local 5.6%
- Federal 14.5%
- Other 37.0%

Source: U.S. National Center for Education Statistics (1977a), p. 22-23.

[1] Excludes an estimated $62 million by public, and $39 million by private, subcollegiate departments of institutions of higher education.

Structure of Governance

The governance of American colleges and universities has been characterized as "a residue of traditions and arrangements that are more the gift of history than of conscious thought."[15] At the campus level, at least four actors are important: boards of trustees; presidents (and other institutional administrators); faculty; and students. Most outside observers recognize the distinctive importance in the United States of university presidents and of lay boards of trustees (regents). In public institutions, the boards are typically appointed by elected state officials such as governors or legislators or—in the case of many community college districts—elected by local citizens.[16] In the private sector, boards of trustees are self-perpetuating in terms of their membership and are usually charged by charter with the total welfare of the institution. Trustees select and delegate administrative authority to the president. Whether public or private, the board of trustees is frequently subject to external nongovernmental forces such as alumni and professional associations, economic interest groups, and private foundations.

In the United States, the power and influence of individuals and groups—both on and off campus—is complex and changing. Especially at the level of the intrainstitutional departments, faculty maintain considerable individual and collegial control over curriculum, research, promotion, and tenure decisions. Faculty also participate in decision making through academic senates and faculty councils although influence at levels above the department varies a great deal from campus to campus. Collective bargaining is rapidly emerging as a significant mechanism for faculty influence, and encompasses budgetary as well as other matters. By July 1975, faculty bargaining had been organized on 431 campuses and contracts had been negotiated on 360 campuses.[17]

With the expansion of elective courses and a decline in the *in loco parentis* approach, student groups have been increasingly influential. However, while students often serve on academic committees and on other governing boards, "student influence is largely confined to nonacademic matters in which students have traditionally had some voice."[18] When student organizations and groups were formed to demonstrate on racial issues in the late sixties and against the Vietnam war in the early seventies, their voice was clearly heard. In many institutions they gained seats on higher governing bodies. But today, there appears to be less interest among student groups in exercising their influence; instead they have turned toward academic concerns and intensified competition.

Boards of trustees, presidents, and other senior campus administrators retain a good deal of power over budgetary and academic policies including admission, student life, personnel decisions (e.g., appointments of faculty), sponsored research, and other matters vital to the well-being of the institutions. As a result of increased enrollment and other factors, the number of multicampus boards and executives has grown dramatically in recent years. Table 8 shows the pattern of campus governance in senior public institutions of higher education in 1975.[19]

In the post-World War II period, the role of the federal government expanded along with funding for student aid, physical facilities, research, and the development of medical, engineering, and scientific manpower. States, however, have retained the basic responsibility for public education at all levels. Many observers feel the most striking shift in the distribution of power within higher education since the early 1960s has been toward "superboards," state legislatures, and governors.[20] In 1975, twenty-two states had consolidated governing boards for all public senior, and sometimes junior, institutions. In thirteen of these states, consolidated governing boards also bear responsibility for coordination of all, or a substantial portion of, public institutions of higher education (Table 9). Twenty-eight states have state coordinating councils or agencies, two-thirds of which have important regulatory authority.

TABLE 8
Patterns of Campus Governance of Public Senior
Institutions of Higher Education, 1975

Governing Body	Number
Individual Campus Boards [1]	5
Multicampus Boards[2]	8
Consolidated Boards[3]	22
Mixed Pattern[4]	15
Total States	50

Source: Various sources cited in Carnegie Foundation for Advancement of Teaching (1976a), p. 89.
[1] Individual boards govern each public senior institution. The University of Kentucky also governs thirteen two-year colleges. The University of Michigan board governs three campuses of the system. The University of Missouri is responsible for four campuses.
[2] The typical pattern is two or more multicampus boards (e.g., state universities, and state colleges), some of which also have jurisdiction over two-year institutions.
[3] More than one state has separate institution boards with delegated powers from the central, consolidated board responsible for all public senior institutions.
[4] Separate boards for some senior institutions and multicampus boards for others.

In 1972, Congress amended Title XII of the Higher Education Act of 1965 to authorize designation of a new or existing state agency as the State Postsecondary Education Commission (Sec. 1202) to receive funds under Section 1203 for "Comprehensive Statewide Planning" for postsecondary education, and to receive

TABLE 9

Patterns of State Coordination of Public Institutions of Higher Education, 1975

Coordinating Body	Number
Consolidated Governing Board	13[1]
Advisory[2] Coordinating Agency	9
Regulatory[2] Coordinating Agency	19
No Overall Coordination	9[3]
Total States	50

Source: Various sources cited in Carnegie Foundation for the Advancement of Teaching (1976a), p. 90; and *Chronicle of Higher Education* (1976).

[1] South Dakota has no public, two-year colleges, Wisconsin has a separate state board for vocational, technical, and adult education; Rhode Island has a separate junior college state system.

[2] A coordinating board or agency is designated as "regulatory" if it has authority over one or more important aspects of higher education, such as the right to approve programs or to present a single consolidated budget for public postsecondary education.

[3] In six states, consolidated governing boards for senior institutions do coordinate them; the consolidated board in Vermont is also responsible for the state's single statewide community college. Two of the nine states have separate state boards for community colleges. The State Department of Education governs (and coordinates) two-year institutions in five states. Only Nebraska has no coordinating board or agency.

TABLE 10

Type of 1202 Commission, by State Board or Agency for Higher Education, 1975-76

State Coordinating or Governing Board	Total	Existing or Augmented Board	New	None
Coordinating	28	23	3	2
Consolidated	19	8	9	2
No Board	3	—	3	—
Total States	50	31	15	4

Source: Carnegie Foundation for the Advancement of Teaching (1976b), p. 53.

and distribute funds subsequently appropriated under a new Title X (Community Colleges and Occupational Education).[21] By law the "1202 Commissions" are to be "broadly and equitably" representative of *all* public and private institutions of postsecondary education, including public noncollegiate and proprietary schools.

Of the forty-six states taking advantage of funds appropriated since 1974 under Section 1203, thirty-one chose an existing sometimes augmented agency—often the state coordinating council for higher education—to serve as the state postsecondary education commission (Table 10). The remaining fifteen established a new agency. Four states—Colorado, North Carolina, Tennessee, and Wisconsin—decided not to take advantage of the 1203 funds.

With respect to private sector institutions offering occupational programs below the baccalaureat—"proprietaries" and nonprofit institutions, such as the many hospital schools of nursing—the 1202 Commissions provide a mechanism through which the private sector can associate with public policy at the state level. The same is true for senior private institutions of higher education, but in this case the voice is not a new one, since the concerns of private higher education in many states have been channeled, to a degree, through existing statewide coordinating agencies and state scholarships and loan commissions.

Purposes and Goals

Higher education, like every social institution and social process, must be concerned with ends and means. Sometimes this point-counterpoint is described as goals and purposes, and sometimes as functions and instruments. The Carnegie Commission, in *The Purposes and Performance of Higher Education in the United States*,[22] drew a distinction between "purposes," as intentions or end goals such as student learning, and "functions," as instruments for achieving goals. Various terms—aims, purposes, goals, or "enduring aspirations"[23] are often used interchangeably. Most writers, however, attempt to distinguish between ultimate ends and more instrumental objectives necessary to their attainment. Furthering democratic reforms and social mobility would be examples of the former; financial aid to students or expansion of enrollment opportunities typify the latter. In this sense, the major activities of higher education—teaching, research, and public service—are seen as functions.

In the United States, the subject is further complicated by the wide diversity among institutions. While many could agree in general on their goals and purposes, there would be greater differences in their functions, their ways of approaching their aims. It is frequently observed that not all colleges and universities should be expected to perform all functions. This is a recurrent theme and a source of strength for the higher education system in our country. We have many students of widely varying abilities and interests, spread out over a very large country. Our diversity is vital in serving the people's needs.

Moreover, at various times in our history, greater emphasis has been placed on different goals. When we were a developing country, a small elite group was educated; later, education was diversified and extended to private training in agriculture and technical skills. In the 1950s (the Sputnik Era) both the Rockefeller Report on Education[24] and the Joseph's Committee Report [25] gave considerable attention to society's need for more scientists, engineers, and teachers.

Without pretending to review the literature on goals or purposes comprehensively, the following may be helpful.[26]

Equality of Educational Opportunity. This goal is sometimes expressed in terms of access, with attention to geography, income, and barriers associated with social class, sex, race, creed, or national origin. Nearly all expressions of this, often proximate, goal emphasize that opportunity should be consistent with the aptitude and interests of prospective students. Identifying and nurturing talent, ensuring social justice, and reducing social tension are sometimes considered more ultimate ends.

As Trivett has noted, since World War II nearly all statements of purpose in higher education have emphasized equality of opportunity.[27] For example, in 1947 the U.S. President's Commission on Higher Education (Truman Commission) stated:[28]

> The American people should set as their ultimate goal an education system in which at no level—high schools, college, graduate school, or professional school—will a qualified individual in any part of the country encounter an insuperable economic barrier to the attainment of the kinds of education suited to his aptitudes and interests.
>
> Equal educational opportunity for all persons, to the maximum of their individual abilities and without regard to economic status, race, creed, color, sex, national origin, or ancestry is a major goal of American democracy. Only an informed, thoughtful, tolerant people can maintain and develop a free society.

President Johnson drew major attention to equality of opportunity when he signed the Higher Education Act of 1965:[29]

> To thousands of young men and women, this act means the path of knowledge is open to all who have the determination to walk it.... It is the obligation of your nation to provide and permit and assist every child born in these borders to receive all the education that he can take.

In recent years, nontraditional forms of higher education—particularly as these relate to lifelong learning—have received special attention with respect to equality of opportunity. A 1971 report on higher education by the Office of Education stressed that "the time has come to halt academic lock-step and reconstitute our colleges and universities as educational institutions for individuals of all ages."[30]

Meeting Manpower Needs. While educators and politicians generally agree that equality of opportunity must be provided, there is recurrent controversy over the goal of meeting manpower needs. Essentially, the debate revolves around whether manpower needs should guide decisions regarding the expansion of higher education, or whether the choice of individuals—for example, to attend college and select their own field of study—should be the decisive factors. Government and public policy statements generally stress the former. Of course, in a democratic society no one can coerce students to study for a certain career, so the debate is somewhat rhetorical.

Still it is not without influence. While the federal government cannot and should not control numbers to fit projected manpower needs, it can and does support training in pertinent fields, as it has in science and research. On the state level, manpower requirements have been considered when decisions are made on graduate programs to be offered or expanded. For example, the New York State Regents have denied approval for institutions to start new programs in fields where there is already an oversupply of trained personnel. As the Regents stated in a 1972 report:[31]

> Higher education should allow a meshing of the students' aspirations and abilities for higher education, the availability of academic and professional programs, and the needs of society as manifested by career opportunities.

The issue is further complicated in the United States because we have no central office for statistics and projections. The National

Science Foundation, the Bureau of Labor Statistics, and the National Center for Educational Statistics issue data and advice but the projections are either limited to selected occupations or too general to be of great use in the formulation of educational policy. There is no one infallible source—if such is even possible or desirable in a free economy based on individualism. Predictions and media reports do, however, inform the people as they make their own decisions.

Since the goals of higher education are certainly broader than just meeting manpower needs or training persons directly for employment, college and university educators generally consider this goal as only one of several purposes and not the first in priority. Of course, institutions established for vocational purposes see the issue in reverse: training for manpower needs is a first purpose. So the United States muddles along with this goal, which none fully deny, but about which we differ on means and functions.

General Improvement of Society. The members of the Truman Commission viewed this goal as the single most important function of higher education.[32]

> Perhaps [higher education's] most important role is to serve as an instrument of social transition, and its responsibilities are defined in terms of the kind of civilization society hopes to build. If its adjustments to present needs are not to be mere fortuitous improvisations, those who formulate its policies and programs must have a vision of the nation and the world we want.

But there is no improvement without self-criticism; thus, higher education must produce men and women whose critical views spur society to advance. As a recent Carnegie Commission report put it: "Faculty members and students, as an integral part of their scholarly activities, should have both the freedom and the opportunity to engage in the evaluation of society through individual thought and persuasion."[33] Beyond functioning as a social critic, traditional higher education also serves to improve society by acquainting students with the highest and most enduring human values; in this respect, higher education encourages students to want and expect the best from their society. Surely there is no goal for higher education which society as a whole should support more.

Development of the Individual. While individual development is often viewed in relation to equality of opportunity, general improvement of society, and meeting manpower needs, it clearly extends beyond all three. A 1957 report of the National Education Association emphasized the importance of higher education's role in the total development of the individual:[34]

> [higher education's] purpose is to draw out the latent talent of youth, to give opportunity for able youth to mature intellectually, aesthetically, socially, vocationally, and morally.

If the NEA's report had been written today, it would have stressed the significance of this goal for students of all age groups. Certainly, the enormous expansion of adult education programs indicates that individual educational development is a continuing process.

The university or college campus increasingly has found itself—if not with forethought—as the source of creative activity and individual development in intellectual pursuits. While, traditionally, the campus has provided the foundation of learning for future scientists, it has recently been developing a comparable function for artistic endeavors. Scholars of the humanities and social sciences also receive the foundation of their training in the educational establishment.

Individual development of students has always been a foremost goal and probably it is the number one priority for all higher education in the United States—regardless of whether the development was aimed at general education, the sciences or arts, or specific job training.

Advancement and Diffusion of Knowledge. In our country, advancement and diffusion of knowledge have been defined—like other goals—in various ways during different historical periods. Although in general terms everyone agrees that this purpose is central to the purposes of higher education, disagreements arise when shifts in the emphasis or direction of these efforts occur. For example, in the early days of our country's history, advancement and diffusion of knowledge primarily involved instructing gentlemen in the classics and acquainting them with the virtues expected of leaders in society. The latter function often assumed priority during this period, since most of the early colleges and universities were founded by a church or religious group. After World War

II — after university experts had successfully produced the atomic bomb and radar — the university "came to be regarded as the fountainhead of the expanding research necessary to the growth of a technological society."[35] This emphasis on scientific and technolocal advancement continued up until the midsixties, when civil disruptions and widespread disillusionment with technology for its own sake resulted in a growing awareness that education should be, brought "back to earth." Now this trend has reversed itself to some extent.

A new report just published by fifteen university presidents[36] points out the importance of the alignment between the government and major research universities — not only to maintain one of the major purposes of the universities but to ensure that their research activities will be coordinated with the nation's efforts. The alliance will benefit both society and the students trained for the fastest growing fields of science and technology.

Diffusion of knowledge is of course a different issue in part, it goes beyond "advancement" and "new discoveries." Teaching is the major function for diffusion, though research may be stressed on the rationale that it bulwarks good teaching. On this issue, U.S. colleges and universities have one of their greatest arguments at present. We have stressed publications as evidence of research — knowing too often that the publications did not constitute originality, new interpretations, or a contribution to scholarship. But currently many institutions, and especially the smaller liberal arts colleges, where research and publications have been slim, are questioning this purpose. Teaching has too often been neglected in the teachers' efforts to produce print. So current news items indicate questioning of this goal and reassertion of teaching itself as a skill to convey the lively inheritance of the knowledge of past generations to the students of today.

Continuing Education for Adults. A relatively new goal, which is receiving increased attention, is that of providing educational services to meet the recurrent, lifelong learning needs of adults. By the year 2000 it is estimated that approximately 30 percent of the U.S. population will be over fifty years old.[37] This demographic trend is expected to produce significant social, political, and educational change. The traditional pattern, which chopped the individual's life into compartments — so many years for education, so many years for work and retirement — is giving way to a more fluid structure in which work, education, and leisure are mixed to suit the needs of the individual's lifestyle. As Alan Pifer has stated the new societal attitude:[38]

> Education [should] be seen not just as preparation for life but as part of life itself, to be enjoyed simply as recreation or for its ability to enhance human understanding and capability over the entire life cycle.

This shift in the population's age structure has already had political ramifications. In 1965, Congress established a special agency to deal with the needs of its senior citizens. The Administration on Aging was originally administered under the Social and Rehabilitation Service Agency; then as a result of the Older Americans Comprehensive Service Amendments passed in 1973, it was moved under the direct control of the Department of Health, Education, and Welfare. The budget for the Administration on Aging increased from $7 million in 1966 to $227.8 million in 1974 — a clear indication of political support.[39]

Although community colleges have made the greatest effort to respond to the educational needs of adults in their communities, large public and private universities are also beginning to gear programs toward the needs of older students. For example, Ohio State University now offers "Program 65," which admits students sixty-five years old and over to certain courses in five of the university's colleges; admission to the courses is based on the availability of space and is free-of-charge to adult students. Other similar programs are being offered at the University of Cincinnati, the University of Pittsburgh, Roosevelt University, Fairleigh Dickinson University, the University of Chicago, the University of Tulsa, and the University of Kentucky among others.[40] The admission of adults to institutions of higher education is expected to increase dramatically in the coming years and, more than any other single factor, may produce the most far reaching changes in higher education as it is practiced in the United States.

Community Service. The concept of community service as a purpose of higher education may have grown out of the extension courses provided by the land grant colleges, authorized under the 1862 Morrill Act. From an international perspective, it is a relatively unusual purpose. Very few educational systems include community service as one of their stated functions.

From the training of clergymen and statesmen, however, this function has a long tradition in the United States; a democracy cannot grow without cooperation and service for others. Nor, perhaps, can it be maintained without these attributes. Further, the fact that public monies from tax dollars go toward education justifies this service in the public's mind.

With the authorization of Title I of the Higher Education Act in 1965, the government, under Lyndon Johnson, gave support to the concept. Besides the role played by community colleges, some of the large public and private universities have also joined the effort.[41] For example, the University of Chicago has conducted several programs to revitalize slum areas in south Chicago. Through the Woodlawn-Model Cities Plan, it has sponsored community mental health, child care, and drug abuse centers and has donated financial credits toward housing rehabilitation and construction. The Area Services Plan, created in 1965 by Southern Illinois University, became a primary force for the renewal of mining cities in southern Illinois. The university encouraged self-help programs and provided leadership and staff. The plan was instrumental in renovating local government buildings and in attracting new industries to the cities.

Morgan State College in Maryland created a precedent setting program to train inner-city school teachers in 1965. The college sent 150 students as interns to inner-city schools in Baltimore. The students selected as interns were paid $135 a month and were required to commit themselves to two years of teaching in inner-city schools after graduation. Northeastern University in Boston was one of the first universities to create cooperative education programs; since the turn of the century, it has been serving working-class students and providing courses which combine education with work and earned income. Yale University has programs for the elderly, housing rehabilitation, legal assistance to poorer communities, seminars for city teachers, and through its Hill-Health Center is currently training ambulance workers and a special emergency cardiac team. Similar programs are being created in almost every major college and university across the nation.

Goals and purposes of higher education in the United States have not generally been officially expressed except in terms of specific legislation and presidential statements. While each president since Harry Truman has appointed a task force on higher education, their reports have not received great attention. Our goals and functions, then, have evolved and changed in response to changing needs. A sort of consensus exists among institutions concerning the general scope of higher education's efforts, but individuality is preserved within the diversity of our systems.

FOOTNOTES

1. U.S. National Center for Education Statistics, 1976. Unless otherwise indicated, tables and charts in this paper exclude institutions in "outlying areas," which include American Samoa, Canal Zone, Guam, Puerto Rico, the Virgin Islands, and the Trust Territory of the Pacific Islands. An institution of higher education is defined as one offering at least a two-year program of college level studies creditable toward an associate or higher degree. See: U.S. National Center for Education Statistics, *The Condition of Education, 1976 Edition* (Washington, D.C.: Government Printing Office, 1976), p. ix for additional details.
2. U.S. National Center for Education Statistics, *Digest of Education Statistics: 1976 Edition* (Washington, D.C.: Government Printing Office, 1977), p. 105.
3. The basis for distinguishing between doctoral-granting institutions (research universities I and II, and other doctoral-granting institutions) and between liberal arts I and II is described in: Carnegie Commission on Higher Education, *A Classification of Institutions of Higher Education. A Technical Report* (Berkeley, California: Carnegie Commission on Higher Education, 1973). Among the former, institutions were ranked according to number of Ph.D.s awarded and federal financial support of academic science. Size and nature of program offerings distinguish comprehensive colleges and universities. Liberal arts I embraces highly selective liberal arts colleges as measured by Astin's selectivity index, or as ranked by the National Academy of Sciences.
4. Many are branches of multicampus community colleges, often located in large urban areas (e.g., Cleveland, Ohio; Dade County (Miami), Florida; and Dallas, Texas). Others are two-year branches of state universities—a pattern not atypical in states such as Pennsylvania and Ohio.
5. The reader can make similar comparisons by locating values along each axis at any point on the three curves.
6. Less than fifty independent, nondegree-granting private institutions are proprietary (profit-seeking). See: U.S. National Center for Education Statis-

tics, *The Condition of Education, 1976 Edition* (Washington, D.C.: Government Printing Office, 1976), p. xxix.
7. U.S. National Center for Education Statistics, *Projections of Educational Statistics to 1975-76* (Washington, D.C.: Government Printing Office, 1966), p. 20; U.S. National Center for Education Statistics, *Digest of Education Statistics: 1976 Edition* (Washington, D.C.: Government Printing Office, 1977), p. 81. Ninety-two percent of the total are enrolled in public, two-year institutions (*Ibid.*, p. 87).
8. Such schools offer programs *not* generally creditable toward a baccaluareate degree. Many are accredited, however, and students are eligible for selected forms of student financial assistance (e.g.), federally insured loans).
9. U.S. National Center for Education Statistics, *The Condition of Education, 1977 Edition*, Vol. III, Part I, a Statistical Report (Washington, D.C.: Government Printing Office, 1977), p. 179.
10. *Ibid.*, p. 185.
11. U.S. National Center for Education Statistics, *Digest of Education Statistics: 1976 Edition* (Washington, D.C.: Government Printing Office, 1977) p. 25.
12. *Ibid.*, p. 184. On-campus students also paid an additional $1,200 or so for room and board in 1974-75, the latest year for which such statistics have been published (*Ibid.*, p. 155).
13. Expenditures by the Carnegie classification of institutions is not available. "The designation "universities," as used by the U.S. National Center for Education Statistics, includes many institutions labeled, "comprehensive colleges and universities" in the Carnegie typology.
14. The fraction would be larger if account were taken of veteran's benefits and other student financial assistance not administered by campuses. Such funds show up, in part, as income from "other" sources, such as revenue from auxiliary enterprises and student fees.
15. Clark Kerr, "Governance and Function," *Daedalus*, 99 (1), Winter, 1970, p. 108.
16. See, for example: Kerr, *Ibid.;* and B.R. Clark and T.I.K. Youn, *Academic Power in the United States: Comparative Historic and Structural Perspectives*. ERIC/Higher Education Research Report No. 3 (Washington, D.C.: American Association for Higher Education, 1976).
17. U.S. National Center for Education Statistics. *The Condition of Education, 1976 Edition* (Washington, D.C.: Government Printing Office, 1976), p. 253.
18. L.H. Robinson and J.D. Shoenfeld, *Student Participation in Academic Governance*. A report of the ERIC Clearinghouse on Higher Education (Washington D.C.: ERIC, The George Washington University, 1970), p.1.
19. The governance of public two-year colleges tends to be centered more at the local level, in states which rely heavily on local property taxes. On the other hand, many boards for other types of postsecondary institutions have jurisdiction over an entire district. In other states, state boards of education, which are typically responsible for grades K-12, govern. In other states—for example, California, Colorado, Connecticut, and Delaware—separate state-level boards govern two-year campuses. In Alaska, Hawaii, and some other

states, consolidated boards for senior institutions also govern two-year campuses.

20. In its final report, the Carnegie Commission observed: "The great change of the past decade was not the vociferous rise of student power but the quiet increase in public power—by governors, by legislators, by coordinating councils. Some of higher education already has the status of a highly controlled public utility." See: Carnegie Commission on Higher Education, *Priorities for Action: Final Report of the Carnegie Commission on Higher Education* (New York: McGraw-Hill Book Co., 1973) p. 59.

21. Funds for Title X were never appropriated and the "occupational education" section was rescinded with the education amendments of 1976.

22. Carnegie Commission on Higher Education, *The Purposes and Performance of Higher Education in the United States* (New York: McGraw-Hill Book Co., 1973).

23. This term was used by the New York Regents (1971).

24. Rockefeller Brothers Fund, Inc., *The Pursuit of Excellence: Education and the Future of America.* Panel Report V of the Special Studies Project. (Garden City, N.Y.: Doubleday & Co. Inc., 1958).

25. U.S. President's Committee on Education Beyond High School (The Eisenhower or Josephs Committee), *Second Report to the President* (Washington, D.C.: Government Printing Office, July 1957).

26. The order is not intended to imply the relative importance of each. Categories are to some extent arbitrary, and the interconnectedness not always apparent without a careful reading of goal statements. Trivett provides a surcinct review of recent literature. See: D.A. Trivett, *Goals for Higher Education* ERIC/Higher Education Research Report No. 6 (Washington, D.C.: American Association for Higher Education, 1973.)

27. For example, see: U.S. President's Commission on Higher Education (The Truman Commission), *Higher Education for American Democracy* (New York: Harper and Brothers, Publishers, 1947); the Carnegie Commission on Higher Education, *The Purposes and the Performance of Higher Education in the United States* (New York: McGraw-Hill Book Co., 1973), p. 29-30; U.S. President, "The President's Message to the Congress Proposing Measures to Expand Opportunities for Higher Education. February 22, 1971," *Weekly Compilation of Presidential Documents,* Vol. 7 (9), March 1, 1971, p. 280-283; International Commission on the Development of Education (The Faure Commission), *Learning to Be: The World of Education Today and Tomorrow* (Paris: UNESCO, 1972); U.S. Office of Education, *Report on Higher Education (The Newman Report)* (Washington, D.C.: Government Printing Office, March 1971).

28. U.S. President's Commission on Higher Education (The Truman Commission), *Higher Education for American Democracy* (New York: Harper & Brothers, Publishers, 1947), Vol. I, p. 36, Vol. II, p. 3.

29. U.S. President, "Remarks at Southwest Texas State College Upon Signing the Higher Education Act of 1965," *Public Papers of the Presidents of the United States, 1965. Book II* (Washington, D.C.: Government Printing Office, 1965), pp. 1102-1106.

30. U.S. Office of Education, *Report on Higher Education (The Newman Report)* (Washington, D.C.: Government Printing Office, March 1971).
31. New York, Regents of the University of the State of New York. *Education Beyond High School. The Regents Planning Bulletin Concerning the Regents Statewide Plan for Development of Higher Education 1972.* (Albany, N.Y.: Author, 1971.)
32. U.S. President's Commission on Higher Education (The Truman Commission), *Higher Education for American Democracy* (New York: Harper & Brothers, 1947), Vol. I, p. 22.
33. Carnegie Commission on Higher Education, *The Purposes and the Performance of Higher Education in the United States* (1973b), p. 50.
34. National Education Association, Educational Policies Commission. *Higher Education in a Decade of Decision.* (Washington, D.C.: N.E.A. and the American Association of School Administrators, 1957), p. 6.
35. Lewis B. Mayhew, The Carnegie Commission on Higher Education (San Francisco: Jossey Bass, 1973), p. 2.
36. *Research Universities and the National Interest.* A Report From Fifteen University Presidents (New York: copyright Ford Foundation, 1977).
37. *Lifelong Learners—A New Clientele for Higher Education: Current Issues in Higher Education, 1974,* Dyckman W. Vermilye, ed. (San Francisco: Jossey Bass, 1974), p. 7.
38. Alan Pifer, *Women Working: Toward a New Society.* Reprinted from the 1976 Annual Report of the Carnegie Corporation, p. 17.
39. *Never Too Old to Learn.* A Report submitted to the Edna McConnell Clark Foundation by the Academy for Educational Development, June 1974, pp. 12-14.
40. *Ibid,* p. 16.
41. For the following summary of community service programs, I am greatly indebted to a case study of eight public service programs presented in *The University and the City,* edited by George Nash (Berkeley: The Carnegie Commission on Higher Education, 1973) and to David Warren, for outlining the programs currently sponsored at Yale (phone conversation, February 28, 1978).

REFERENCES

Blake, E., Jr., Lambert, L.J., and Martin, J.L. *Degrees Granted and Enrollment Trends in Historically Black Colleges: An Eight Year Study.* ISE Research Report, Vol. 1, No. 1. Washington, D.C.: Institute for Services to Education, October 1974.

Carnegie Commission on Higher Education. *Less Time, More Options: Education Beyond the High School.* New York: McGraw-Hill Book Co., 1971.

———. *A Classification of Institutions of Higher Education.* A Technical Report, Berkeley, Calif.: Author, 1973a.

———. *The Purposes and the Performance of Higher Education in the United States.* New York: McGraw-Hill Book Co., 1973b.

———. *Governance of Higher Education: Six Priority Problems.* New York: McGraw-Hill Book Co., 1973c.

———. *Priorities for Action: Final Report of the Carnegie Commission on Higher Education.* New York: McGraw-Hill Book Co., 1973d.

Carnegie Foundation for the Advancement of Teaching. *More Than Survival: Prospects for Higher Education in a Period of Uncertainty.* A commentary with recommendations. San Francisco: Jossey-Bass Publishers, 1975.

———. *The States and Higher Education.* A commentary with recommendations. San Francisco: Jossey-Bass Publishers, 1976a.

———. *The States and Higher Education. Supplement* to a commentary. Berkeley, Calif.: Carnegie Council on Policy Studies in Higher Education, 1976b.

Chronicle of Higher Education, "Statewide Boards for 2-Year Colleges." Fact-File. Vol. XIII (9), November 1, 1976.

Clark, B.R., and Youn, T. I. K. *Academic Power in the United States: Comparative Historic and Structural Perspectives.* ERIC/Higher Education Research Report No. 3. Washington, D.C.: American Association for Higher Education, 1976.

International Commission on the Development of Education. *Learning to Be: The World of Education Today and Tomorrow.* (The Faure Commission). Paris: UNESCO, 1972.

Kerr, C. "Governance and Function," *Daedalus,* 99 (1), Winter, 1970, pp. 108-121.

Kerr, C. "Ice Age or New Horizons," in *Perspectives for the Future System of Higher Education.* Hiroshima, Japan: Research Institute for Higher Education, Hiroshima University, January 1977, pp. 27-37.

National Education Association, Educational Policies Commission. *Higher Education in a Decade of Decision.* Washington, D.C.: NEA and the American Association of School Administrators, 1957.

New York, Regents of the University of the State of New York. *Education Beyond High School. The Regents Planning Bulletin Concerning the Regents Statewide Plan for Development of Higher Education 1972.* Albany, N.Y.: Author, April 1971.

Robinson, L.H., and Shoenfeld, J.D. *Student Participation in Academic Governance.* A Report of the ERIC Clearinghouse on Higher Education. Washington, D.C. ERIC, The George Washington University, 1970.

Rockefeller Brothers Fund, Inc. *The Pursuit of Excellence: Education and the Future of America.* Panel Report V of the Special Studies Project. Garden City, N.Y.: Doubleday & Co., Inc., 1958.

Trivett, D.A. *Goals for Higher Education.* ERIC/Higher Education Research Report No. 6. Washington, D.C.: American Association for Higher Education, 1973.

U.S. National Center for Education Statistics. *Projections of Educational Statistics to 1975-76.* Washington, D.C.: GPO, 1966.

―――――. *Directory of Postsecondary Schools with Occupational Programs, 1973-74.* Washington, D.C.: GPO, 1975.

―――――. *The Condition of Education, 1976 Edition.* Washington, D.C.: GPO, 1976.

―――――. *Education Directory: Colleges and Universities, 1975-76.* Washington, D.C.: GPO, 1976a.

―――――. *Digest of Education Statistics: 1976 Edition.* Washington, D.C.: GPO, 1977a.

―――――. *Projections of Education Statistics to 1985-86.* Washington, D.C.: GPO, 1977b.

―――――. *The Condition of Education, 1977 Edition.* Vol. III, Part I, a Statistical Report. Washington, D.C.: GPO, 1977c.

―――――. *Financial Statistics of Institutions of Higher Education: Current Fund Revenues and Expenditures, Fiscal Year 1975, State Data.* Washington, D.C.: GPO, 1977d.

U.S. Office of Education. *Report on Higher Education.* (The Newman Report). Washington, D.C.: GPO, March 1971.

U.S. President. "Remarks at Southwest Texas State College Upon Signing the Higher Education Act of 1965." *Public Papers of the Presidents of the United States,* 1965. Book II, pp. 1102-1106. Washington, D.C.: GPO, 1965.

U.S. President. "The President's Message to the Congress Proposing Measures to Expand Opportunities for Higher Education. February 22, 1971." *Weekly Compilation of Presidentail Documents,* Vol. 7 (9), March 1, 1971, pp. 280-283.

U.S. President's Commission on Higher Education. *Higher Education for American Democracy.* (The Truman Commission). New York: Harper and Brothers, Publishers, 1947.

U.S. President's Committee on Education Beyond High School. *Second Report to the President.* (The Eisenhower or Josephs Committee). Washington, D.C.: GPO, July 1957.

ADMINISTRATION OF HIGHER EDUCATION

David D. Henry

The National Setting

The distinguishing characteristics of higher education in the United States are its diversity and scope. In a strict sense, the term "system" does not apply, for there is no formal structure at the national level for planning, evaluation, finance, policy formulation, or administration. This condition has resulted from the history and nature of the development of postsecondary educational institutions and the massive cumulative effort of those institutions to independently extend educational opportunity to an ever increasing population, with an expanding proportion of citizens—young and old, varied in interests, aspirations, and aptitudes—who have sought what they regard to be the advantages of higher education.

Institutions of higher education in the United States differ with respect to their goals, organization, and governance. They vary in size, resources, methods of financial support, and their constituencies; and they vary in other ways:[1]

> Not only do institutions have widely different structures and purposes, but they have widely different professional autonomy for their faculties. In some instances the faculties are highly professional, determining their own work processes and controlling personnel practices. In other situations the faculty are merely hired employees, and have very little professional autonomy.
>
> The decision processes also vary substantially. Some institutions are dominated by strong presidents. Some have strong

faculty and collegial participation. Some allow students a strong voice in the decision-making process. Some are bound by state system regulations and have little decision-making latitude. Some are virtually dominated by the local communities that they serve. Any adequate understanding of American higher education must take this hodgepodge of institutional styles into account.

To think of the over 3,000 colleges and universities as being of two types—public and private—comprising a "dual system" is an oversimplification. The "system" is multiple. Among publicly controlled institutions are community colleges, urban four-year colleges and universities, regional state colleges, and comprehensive state universities, some of which emphasize the research role. Among privately controlled institutions are two-year colleges, liberal arts colleges, special purpose colleges, comprehensive universities, and nationally oriented research universities. Within the group of small colleges, public and private, some provide a liberal arts curriculum and others offer diversified vocational and professional preparation. The larger research-oriented institutions, with heavy emphasis upon graduate work, are divided evenly between public and private.

Institutions are more comparable in terms of purpose, function, and scope than differences in their method of organization, governance, or sources of support suggest. A large private urban institution that accepts community service as one of its responsibilities is not unlike the municipal or state university located in the metropolitan area. The small liberal arts college of private origin is not unlike the small state college of limited purpose. Moreover, all colleges and universities are also similar in that they serve a public purpose and play a part in the collective service of higher education. Further, all institutions must search for resources to carry out their purposes effectively and to present programs of quality— however the individual institution defines its own goals.

Before 1930, the growth of institutions in number, size, and complexity had been fairly steady but slow paced over a period of sixty years. After 1930, with dips in the depression years of the thirties, the World War II period, and the early fifties, enrollments increased more rapidly. In the 1960s, the surge of enrollments accelerated, even ahead of the population growth. This expansion to what may be called "mass enrollment" was unprecedented in the

United States and may be traced to the popular faith that higher education provides a means toward social mobility, career preparations, and personal development. Fortunately, the timing was right, the demand arose in a period of economic expansion and financial capability. The expectations, however, and the effort to fulfill them by institutions, were unrelated to any formal national planning. They grew out of the general acceptance that higher education is important to the welfare of the nation through its contributions to an informed citizenry, to the preparation of those who staff the technical and professional services in the nation's life and who serve as leaders in public affairs.

The federal government's involvement in the growth of higher education before the 1960s was indirect, related only to the government's using higher education for specific federal purposes. By law and tradition, the responsibility for education has been left to the states and to private constituencies; hence, no mandate to the federal government for developing higher educaton *per se* exists. The executive and legislative agencies of the federal government have had a benign influence upon colleges and universities and, until recently, have felt that formal responsibility for overall institutional welfare was inappropriate.

However, the land grant colleges were established through federal initiative to encourage industry and agriculture, although many spokesmen for the Land-Grant movement were equally concerned with the benefits to people and to an education broader than that for "agriculture and the mechanic arts." In the depression years, construction grants were made to provide employment, not primarily to help institutions. After World War II, veterans were assisted to go to college because the government had a responsibility for the readjustment of veterans to civilian life, but relatively little attention was given to helping institutions meet the subsequent increases in enrollment. All of these federal actions, and others, had significant impact upon colleges and universities, enlarging their role and creating a climate which encouraged stated governments and benefactors to follow up with support for higher education. The G.I. Bill, for example, had many important educational outcomes and induced desirable change in institutional practice. The incentive, however, was not the strengthening of higher education but the fulfilling of a federal responsibility.

After World War II, the increasing national concern with

scientific advancement moved the government to accept greater responsibility for research, including the preparation of scientists. Even here, however, the institutions were considered as instruments for federal purposes. The term "higher education" did not come into the titles of federal legislation until the Higher Education Facilities Acts of 1963 and 1965; still, the programs that emerged from these measures were specifically limited to ad hoc categories.

Hence, because the federal government has not had and does not now have an overall policy for direct noncategorical federal involvement in higher education, planning for future development — which might be justified in view of the total support now given and sought for higher education activities — is not expected, although there are advocates of a more centralized federal role. Certain provisions of the 1972 amendments to the Higher Education Act seem to point toward the formation of a general national policy, but none of the programs specified in the amendments have been fully funded. Of importance in the future, however, is that this legislation implies that the federal government should accept some responsibility for the financing of higher education beyond student aid and the research function.

Although federal expenditures related to higher education have been unevenly distributed, fragmented, uncoordinated, often below authorizations, without assurance of continuity, and with some of the actions and their corollary regulations threatening the traditional independence of the institutions, the federal involvement has, nevertheless, been of tremendous assistance to higher education institutions in carrying out their collective mission. The academic research establishment, for example, has been enlarged and strengthened. Financial aid to students — in gigantic proportions — has widened the enrollment base and dramatically extended educational opportunity. Specific aspects of institutional performance have been enhanced — the physical plant, libraries, study centers in designated areas such as international education, the health professions, teacher education, the international exchange of students, and public health training, to name a few. We should also mention the Fund for the Improvement of Postsecondary Education, which has encouraged experimentation in significant ways. With all of the criticism of the inconsistencies, inadequacies, unfairness, unequal distribution of federal support, and of the intrusiveness of "federal control," it is generally believed that the federal actions have been of benefit to the "system" and have served the national welfare. However, none of these efforts has emerged from any comprehensive national planning or indeed with much assessment of the impact of federal involvement upon the institutions aided.

Without an overall federal policy, or even of a national consensus on what the role of the federal government toward higher education as a whole should be, the absence of national planning or a national planning mechanism is not surprising. Nor is any consensus to establish national planning encouraged by the sentiment of the academic community, as far as it can be measured. With faculty and administrators restive about and resistant to present excessive federal regulations governing institutional life and with a national mood pressing for some limitation upon the size and influence of the federal bureaucracy, there is little likelihood that the condition will change. A proposed national foundation for the improvement of postsecondary education foundered in part on an inability to define whose ideas for "improvement" were to be controlling. The most that is now generally hoped for is that what has been started in specific ways will be continued and enlarged.

However, the rather dramatic changes that have occurred in higher education in the United States since World War II have not come about as haphazardly as this description might indicate. Efforts have been made, both from the encouragement of federal and state government departments and voluntary organizations, to bring the purposes, goals, needs, and possible new directions of higher education into national focus. Recommendations from voluntary alignments of institutions and those formulated by national associations of institutions and academic personnel have played a significant role in encouraging planning by institutions, states, and private constituencies.

The Report of the President's Commission on Higher Education (the so-called Truman Commission, established in 1947) presented a bold, comprehensive, and new approach for the development of higher education. Although controversial at the time, in the twenty years following most of the philosophical positions of the report were accepted and a majority of the recommendations were, at least, in part adopted. There was a similar response to the recommendations of the President's Committee on Education Beyond the High School (the Eisenhower Committee) established in 1956. The Commission on Financing Higher Education, created in 1952 under the aegis of the Association of American Universities and with the support of the Rockefeller Foundation, had considerable impact, as had the Carnegie Commission on Higher Education (1967-1974), whose studies and recommendations contributed to the national impetus for institutional and state planning. The National Board on Graduate Education (1972-1975), the study programs of the National Science Foundation, and the National Foundation for the Arts and Humanities, have had similar success with smaller scale efforts. The usefulness of the studies, reports, and recommendations of these and other bodies has been determined by nationwide discussion and resulting consensus—not by government direction—and by the voluntary alignment of institutions on the basis of recommendations that have appealed to them as worthy of adoption.

As federal expenditures for higher education have increased, now supporting over 400 programs, there is mounting general interest in coordination and planning of federal activities. Nevertheless, this interest is not directed toward federal coordination of institutions but toward the network of government channels of expenditure for scientific purposes. National decision-making power with respect to higher education is now scattered among most of the federal executive departments, with major responsibilities vested in the departments of health, education, welfare, defense, agriculture, and labor, and the National Science Foundation. The National Foundation for the Arts and the Humanities, the Veteran's Administration, the Atomic Energy Commission, and the National Aeronautic and Space Administration have also played significant roles, as have the departments of state, commerce, justice, and transportation. The involvement of the Corporation for Public Broadcasting, and the Department of Housing and Urban Development and the Department of the Interior has been more limited. When the budgets for these units reach the Congress, they are assigned to different committees, both in the House of Representatives and in the Senate. At no point, either in the administration or in the Congress, is there a coordinated view of federal relations to higher education.

In recent years, the Federal Interagency Committee on Education has been formed, consisting of participants from twenty-nine offices and departments and chaired by the assistant secretary for education from the Department of Health, Education, and Welfare. The committee has performed useful services, particularly in providing information of common interest, but its recommendations have limited force. Each member reports to his own administrative head and the committee's role is therefore necessarily one of communication rather than leadership.

Many of those who study the relationships of the federal government to higher education believe that some high-level central body should have purview over federal activities in this area, with authority to make recommendations for continuing and expanded financial support, and with the mandate to bring recommendations to the attention of the President and to be a point of central contact for the Congress. For many years, some have believed that an independent department of education might effectively carry out such responsibilities and thus bring some order out of the present dispersion. Others, skeptical of the political leverage of such a department, prefer a council of presidential advisors, comparable in function to the Council of Economic Advisors. Such a council could have influence with the President, the departments, and the Congress. However, neither of these nor similar proposals, such as the reorganization of the Department of Health, Education, and Welfare—to give greater identity and prominence to education—has been accepted politically. The welfare of the colleges and universities and the significance of the federal impact upon them has had a low priority among political concerns. Currently, however, both in the administration and among some congressional leaders, there is renewed interest in the establishment of a department of education whose jurisdiction would include federal relations with higher education.

To understand how the "system" of higher education operates in the United States, with particular reference to planning, as related to governance and administration, one must turn to the states and the constituencies of private institutions—for the management of higher education takes place at this, rather than the federal, level. Here again, there is no common pattern, but at the state, regional, and local levels arrangements are less complex and more visible.

Governance and Management

Since higher education in the United States has evolved as a collection of independently managed institutions, one can understand its structure only by examining the governance, operation, and administration of the various institutions. Recent changes that have brought colleges and universities together—for planning purposes and sometimes for mutual service and joint action—should also be considered.

Nearly all nonproprietary colleges and universities have governing boards whose members are entirely or predominantly from occupational and professional fields other than education. The names vary—trustees, regents, and governors, for example—but under the typical state charter, the board is designated as the corporate entity of the institution. The board members come from all walks of life, although those with business or professional backgrounds are in the majority. Most are college graduates, and many are alumni of the institutions they serve. Within the last twenty years, deliberate efforts have been made to bring persons with even more varied backgrounds to the membership of the boards. However, representation of specific constituencies has not controlled selection, although some institutions that are church-related or were affiliated with a church have retained certain religious prescriptions. The trend, however, has been away from such restriction.

The governing boards of colleges and universities in the United States have a more dominant role than have similar groups in most countries. By charter, the boards are usually empowered with ultimate responsibility and authority for their respective institution, but they exercise that authority and fulfill that responsibility in widely varied ways.

Most governing boards consider their role to be policy formulation, prudent trusteeship of financial affairs, and continuing evaluation of the total enterprise. In many instances, however, boards have become directly involved in administration, usually with unhappy consequences. Sometimes boards have tolerated mediocre administrative performance and sometimes they have been unwilling to accept the responsibility for financial procurement. Overall, however, most students of higher education believe the arrangement has been successful.

Lay boards are a bridge between the constituency of the college or university and the institution. The public interest in the examination of goals and purposes, scope, effectiveness, and quality has been well served. Lay boards have also been a bulwark against improper external pressure and interference and have in general been strongly in support of academic freedom and institutional autonomy. At the same time, they have reflected the public interest and have been a means of insuring realistic contact with public expectations.

In 1976, the total membership of the governing boards of some 3,000 colleges and universities, including community colleges, was estimated to exceed 47,000. The members, as citizen volunteers and leaders with diverse experience and background, are collectively a tremendous force in maintaining public confidence in higher education. Many critics of the boards cite examples of inappropriate intrusion in academic affairs and social insensitivity, but the total effect of lay boards leads to the conclusion that they have been a great asset in strengthening the system.[2]

Another distinguishing feature of the management of colleges and universities in the United States is the use of professional administrators, although nearly all administrative personnel come from previous academic employment. Administrative appointments are usually made on a continuing basis, but without tenure or long-term contract. This is particularly true in administrative service beyond the academic department—as college dean, division head, vice-president, president, or chancellor. The same arrangement applies to the service of administrative support personnel—in resource procurement, financial affairs, legal counsel, plant maintenance, and institutional relations.

As colleges and universities have become larger and more complex, the number of career administrators has increased. The development of auxiliary student services on a broader basis has increased staff significantly. Expanding state and federal regulations has been an important factor in the increase in administrative service. The regulations cover a wide range—for example, health and safety conditions, stipulations for research grants, financial audits, municipal and regional planning, labor relations, "affirmative action" in employment, rights of privacy, student loans, civil rights, litigation, and purchasing procedures. Professional training programs now exist for those who choose to prepare for administration and to enter institutional service directly rather than through teaching appointments.

The growth in the professional management of higher education has been a major influence upon institutional planning and development. Institutional programs take years to formulate, requiring extensive involvement with faculty, students, alumni, and the public. A still longer period is required for implementation, including finding the resources. The rotating administrator may manage successfully during a time of limited change; but when adaptation to rapid social and educational change is a major characteristic of the educational scene, expert and committed administrators are required for long-term planning and fulfillment of plans. Administrative initiative, creativity, and "follow-through" are essential.

Although governance and administration are structured in what appears to be an authoritarian hierarchal design—with board, chief executive, deputy administrators, and so on—decision making within the college or university is a shared process, with faculty having a dominant influence on issues directly related to teaching and research. The faculty usually has a campus-wide representative body to deal with educational questions pertaining to admissions, curriculum, calendar, procedures for promotion, working conditions, graduation requirements, academic appointments and promotion, and student affairs. In a large university, the college has comparable machinery for faculty action. The governing board has final authority on all institutional actions, either through delegation or by specific final approval. In actual practice, however, in areas of the kind mentioned, faculty judgment is dominant and usually prevails. When the governing board does not agree in a specific instance, the board is on the defensive and is expected to state its reasons for the decision and be open to continuing evaluation of the consequences.

In some matters, such as budget and long-range planning, the faculty voice is heard and is influential but not necessarily controlling. Nonacademic employment, for example, may follow a civil service procedure in which the faculty is only moderately involved. Institutional budgets begin with requests of the academic departments, but they are subject to administrative evaluation (with faculty consultation), and equity and adequacy are determined finally by the board of control.

On still other subjects, the faculty is only advisory. Goals and purposes, for example, are heavily influenced by the institution's charter and history, overall capabilities, and the public environment. Final judgments on these points are made by the governing board, with professional advice from administration. The scope of the enterprise is also a fundamental question for the constituency ultimately to determine through its representatives, the governing board. The addition of a new college or new program cannot rest entirely on the judgment of the faculty, although faculty opinion, particularly as to the impact of a new program on current operations, is an important point of consideration.

Campus life, including student discipline and parietal rules, was at one time a faculty responsibility. On the current scene, however, these concerns have shifted largely to the administrative officers. Also, the task of disciplining students has in many ways moved from the campus to the courts (other than on problems related to grading and academic evaluation). Because of the emergence of unions, employee relations are generally handled by administrators, particularly in the nonacademic sphere. The recent appearance of collective bargaining for faculty raises the question of the impact of unionization on the traditional faculty governance system and on administrative relations in general.

Another item on the agenda of possible changes in the governing structure is the extent to which students should be formally involved as members of governing boards or of campus administrative and academic committees. Because of their inexperience and the limited time they spend at an institution, the potential contribution of students to management deliberations is necessarily restricted. More serious, however, is the fact that students represent a special group rather than the general citizenry and thus do not meet the usual criteria for formal participation in governance. On the other hand, faculties, administration, and governing boards are sensitive to the necessity for and desirability of an adequate student voice in institutional decisions. The traditional indifference on this point is open to justified criticism. Whether the new mechanisms now being tried are effective or will last remains to be seen.

Faculty involvement at the board level, except through structured advisory committees, has also not been generally favored. As with students, faculty members represent a special group, a criterion not applied to other board members. In both instances, moreover, there is the constant temptation for students or faculty to bypass administrative channels, a practice that invites unfortunate results in orderly management.

While this outline of governing board, administration, and faculty decision making is general, it should be obvious that decision-making procedures vary greatly from the small residential college to the large comprehensive university, to the university system, and finally to the state system. The main components of the structure, however, will be recognizable in every institution, with actual operational differences dependent upon local tradition, administrative styles, faculty strength, and the nature of the institution's mission. In student relations, for example, variations will be influenced by the kinds of students attracted—as reflected in their academic aspirations, their orientation to career development, their social backgrounds, and their life purposes.

During the past thirty years, a new pattern has emerged in the management complex—namely, the multicampus systems. These are under the jurisdiction of overall governing boards, sometimes with unified administration, sometimes with separate campus administration. Although a number of private institutions, for example, New York University, have several geographically dispersed campuses, the campuses are all controlled by the parent institution; the several campuses of public systems, on the other hand, are usually academically autonomous. A number of community college organizations also fall within this category of organization. In size, a number of state systems equal or exceed many national systems.

The best known and one of the earliest examples of the university multicampus system is the University of California, which now has eight general campuses, each with a chancellor and delegated academically autonomous administration. Similarly, the California state colleges, now fourteen in number, are joined under a single board and a unified central administration. The public junior colleges comprise another statewide structure. This "system of systems" in California emerged over a period of time. The earlier campuses of the University of California were considered as branches of the main campus at Berkeley. They developed separate identities, however, and are now considered as educationally autonomous within the system plan; they report through a central administration to the overall board of regents. The state colleges were founded as independent institutions, but, in 1960, were brought together in a multicampus "system." The junior colleges developed in much the same fashion. A similar system of systems recently developed in the 1960s in Illinois. Other examples include the universities of Missouri, Texas, and the City of New York. State coordinating boards also exist in these states.

In another type of state system, all of the public institutions are combined under one governing board with one administrative head, but without any overseeing board or external coordinating board. Systems of this kind have developed recently in North Carolina and Wisconsin. Some states have single governing boards, but they have independent administrations for those campuses that are without central heads. Still other variations—either of a unified state system or a system of systems within a state—also exist.[3]

There are a number of obvious advantages to the multicampus organization as compared with the single independent campus. First, new branch campuses are endowed with the prestige and influence of the institution's older campuses. Some flexibility in internal budgeting is possible, although the degree of such flexibility varies from state to state. Interchange of personnel is possible both in times of growth or of retrenchment. Specialists may be jointly used where duplication is not desirable. Cooperative educational programs and multiple use of educational services are encouraged. In short, there are many educational outcomes that justify the statement that the multicampus system is most valuable in the sense that the whole is greater than the sum of the parts. On the practical side, because the multicampus system is large and therefore more visible, it is more influential with appropriating bodies and agents.

These advantages are not always fully exploited, of course. Faculty relocation during times of economic stringency is resisted. As educational autonomy develops at the separate campuses, at the system level the desired flexibility in resource allocation among campuses is lessened. Flexibility is also lessened by the impingement of outside social or political forces which are not always foreseen in the regular processes of budget analysis and academic planning. Nonetheless, the multicampus arrangement has proven its merit, as attested by the effectiveness and distinction of the largest and better known systems.

The most impressive feature of the multicampus system, particularly important in a time of rapid change and adjustment, is the opportunity for improved institutional planning. Such planning was indispensable in the relatively orderly shifts that made rapid enrollment growth possible and acceptable in the 1960s. Similar advance planning is equally important in dealing with such present uncertainties as changing and shifting enrollments, new program needs, fluctuating markets, distribution of faculty, collective bargaining, and the increasing intrusion of state and federal government agencies, including coordinating boards, into the internal affairs of institutions. As the multicampus arrangement was an asset in the rapid growth of the educational enterprise in the turbulent last two decades, it remains the strongest instrument for planning for the future of the institutions, and it will certainly influence planning for higher education generally. Even where coordinating boards and other state agencies tend to make unilateral decisions affecting the higher education activity, the multicampus system manages to keep a large degree of its internal planning in the hands of educators.

Lee and Bowen[4] have succinctly summarized the impact of the multicampus organization.

> Academic planning and program review are more comprehensive and of higher quality; budgeting is technically more sophisticated and more sensitive to academic criteria. Multicampus programs are increasing, and faculty personnel planning is being initiated. Student mobility is being facilitated. To be sure, few of these activities are limited to multicampus systems; indeed, the experiences of individual campuses, public and private, offer many lessons for systemwide administrators. But the record is sound. Multicampus systems have made a difference for students, for faculty, and for the educational enterprise of their states. The difference has been positive — more so, we believe, than would have been the case had the policies and decisions described in earlier chapters been the responsibility of single campuses, whether dealing with each other as autonomous institutions or dealing directly with state executive and legislative officials and with coordinating agencies.

Planning and Coordination

At every time of crisis, there is a popular call for improved planning, to ensure that similar conditions will not develop again. The outcry is usually accompanied by bitter criticism of those who are regarded as having failed to anticipate the trends and forces that are considered responsible for the current difficulty. Historically, this reaction has been typical in every kind of public issue—economic depression, international conflict, environmental catastrophy, crime, or civil confrontations—even when the record shows that all too often there have been prophets who have not been heard. It also shows that the enthusiasm for planning is lessened as memories of the crisis fade.

The notion that higher education would benefit from planning—within institutions, interinstitutionally on a state or regional basis, and even nationally—was a prominent topic in the 1930s. The changes thrust upon the colleges and universities by the Depression came with such shocking suddenness that the impact was both demoralizing and damaging. Ad hoc decisions, made on the spur of the moment, were not always wise. One of the "lessons" put forward at the time was the warning that periods of contraction would recur and that institutions should plan for them. In the concern of the moment, it was even suggested that expansion should not exceed what could be supported in a period of depression.[5] Nonetheless, the record of the advancement of planning for higher education in the subsequent two decades is not very impressive.

The general failure in implementing planning within institutions is readily explained. The inauguration of "institutional research" was tardy. As late as the mid-fifties, offices for that purpose were uncommon, even among large universities. Although good examples of comprehensive long-range institutional plans were prepared by several large universities—notably the University of Pennsylvania, Columbia University, New York University, and the University of California—basic data for planning at most institutions were not at hand and were seldom available even when requested by external agencies. During the Depression and the following two decades, institutions were so occupied with reacting to environmental pressures that self-study and analysis on a wide and long-term basis had lower priority in the year-to-year struggle for survival. The effects of the Depression stayed longer with colleges and universities than with other components of the economy, and many of the consequences, such as accelerating capital needs and inadequate faculty salaries, were carried over into the 1950s and early 1960s.

No one assumed the responsibility for initiating interinstitutional planning. Lesiglatures and governors reacted to institutional requests on an incremental ad hoc basis. Voluntary cooperation among institutions sometimes developed around specific problems, but only resulted in joint planning on a continuing basis or in a broad way in a few states.

The 1940s were dominated by World War II, including prewar tensions and uncertainties, national mobilization, and the postwar adjustments. The phenomenal emergency expansion to handle the unanticipated number of veterans returning to higher education was a heroic achievement, but it did not grow out of planning nor did it prepare the way for following years. Even the enrollment surge of the 1960s was not fully appreciated until the late 1950s and again the institutions reacted in independent ways.

As the "tidal wave" of prospective students moved through the secondary schools, however, it became clear that some approach to the problems of higher education would be required, other than *laissez faire* and the cumulative reactions of institutions acting alone. The challenge was not only to enlarge capacity for the new numbers but to do so in a way that would be adequate, well-ordered, and effective. The 1957 report of the President's Committee on Education Beyond the High School keynoted the concern:[6]

Revolutionary changes are occurring in American education of which even yet we are only dimly aware. This nation has been propelled into a challenging new educational era since World War II by the convergence of powerful forces— an explosion of knowledge and population, a burst of technological and economic advance, the outbreak of ideological conflict and the uprooting of old political and cultural patterns on a worldwide scale, and an unparalleled demand by Americans for more and better education.... These forces have created enormously increased educational challenges of which we have not taken full stock and which our educational institutions as a whole are ill-prepared to meet. The gap between this nation's educational needs and its educational effort is widening ominously.

The committee reflected the widespread public opinion that pointed to improved planning as a necessity in meeting the new needs and demands. A "random approach" to public service "may have been sufficient when the need was far less complicated and urgent," the report stated, "but it is wholly inadequate for the individual and social needs of today and tomorrow."[7] Planning now should be broad, built on national, regional, state, and local needs; it should be comprehensive, involving all institutions and all agencies, resulting in integrated or interrelated, flexible, action programs. It should include participation by laymen, both for their contributions and as a means of gaining their interest and support, and it should be based upon adequate information. Although "action cannot always await complete study," the report emphasized "that future planning activity will call for a higher degree of concentration, of sophistication, of mutual respect among the various agencies which provide education beyond the high school, and of mutual understanding and confidence between education and the society it serves, than has been typical in the past. Cooperative planning will do much to offset the dangers of complacency, traditionalism and provincialism."[8]

In short, if the new developments in planning—arising from citizen concern with the financial requirements and the effectiveness of education—are to be productive, they must be based upon a broad view of higher education in the public service, upon facts and analysis rather than custom or bias, upon consultation rather than competition, and upon the ability to evolve adequate machinery for interinstitutional cooperation.

In the late 1950s and early 1960s, the public demand for planning in higher education increased and was widely expressed by both lay and professional forums. State political representatives translated the concern into legislation for the public institutions. Among private institutions, sometimes including geographically related state members, voluntary consortiums grew in number and scope. As has been noted, considerable planning had already taken place among multicampus organizations, and in the public sector arrangements were now extended on a statewide basis through a number of coordinating agencies. By 1976, all the states, except nine, had established planning mechanisms for the state-supported institutions.

With respect to their power, authority, and jurisdiction, these agencies—generally called boards, committees, councils, or commissions—may be classified in four categories. Some are advisory only, reporting findings and recommendations to the state authorities—the governor, the legislature, and state departments and bureaus concerned—and to the institutions. Some include both regulatory and advisory functions. Some are in effect boards of control, with mandates to approve budgets and new programs and to implement approved state plans. Finally, there are states in which the boards are all-state governing boards, and hence have responsibility for statewide planning as well as statewide governance.

However the authority and duties of the coordinating board are defined, the power of recommendation, even though advisory, is a significant function. When a recommendation is made in a public forum, the institution is immediately on the defensive if it does not concur. Hence, how that recommendation is formulated and the extent to which the institutions are consulted becomes all important. The behavior of many boards—in acting unilaterally without adequate consultation with the institutions—has often led to divisive public adversary situations. With respect to preserving institutional operational autonomy, relationships between state boards and institutions are delicate at best. Further, some boards have become so involved in implementing initial and partial plans that long-range statewide planning has taken second priority. Also, state boards are often used as agents of the federal government in the promulgation of and reporting upon federal regulations governing the use of federal funds. Governors of the states, too, turn to the state boards for data gathering in response to federal requests. Some state boards serve as 1202 Commissions established by the federal government for grant allocations in certain areas.[9] Hence, although the boards have enormously increased the "paper load" of reports by institutions, some of this is attributable to federal requirements.

Unfortunately, the regulatory approach is inherent in the concept of coordination as viewed by political authorities. Regulation can be particularly deleterious when the boards are staffed by personnel who have limited institutional experience and who are not always sensitive to institutional academic values and standards. Conflict is almost inevitable when political bodies deal with institutions that traditionally have been regarded as immune to political considerations. Perhaps most serious in the long view is the fact that coordinating boards are external to the institutions with which they deal. They are accountable to no constituency, except through political agencies, and they do not have to live on a day-to-day basis with the actions they take. Many students and observers of the practices of state coordinating boards have concluded that unless the coordinating agency is strictly advisory and operates in the spirit of that role—keeping in close consultation with the institutions and observing professional standards in all relationships—it is more desirable to delegate the planning and coordinating responsibility to one overall governing board. A single board is accountable to the people at large as well as to faculty, students, alumni, employers, and others directly involved; it must be sensitive to continuing evaluation of policies and regulations and to the decisions made.

In *The States and Higher Education,* the Carnegie Foundation for the Advancement of Teaching concludes:[10]

> No system of coordination will be fully satisfactory. The problems are too dynamic and the interest groups too diverse. As states search for a more perfect system, the attempted solution is too often directed toward more centralization rather than less. The better answer, however, might lie in a more active market, a more effective budget, a more wisely drawn basic plan, or a higher quality of staff. Each of these possibilities should be explored before further centralization, with its many attendant problems, is chosen as the one and only solution.
>
> Overall, we caution that the external search for small efficiencies and improvements in the short run may kill the spirit of initiative, the self-reliance and the self-responsibility of higher education in the long run and thus, also, lead to major inefficiencies and to deterioration.

Forces other than state-mandated coordination are working to increase voluntary planning both on the part of the individual institution and through interinstitutional cooperation. The Southern Regional Educational Board, representing fourteen states in a compact, has become a model of interstate cooperative planning in higher education. The New England states have established a similar organization, although its history is shorter, the arrangements less formal, and its agenda more limited.

The Committee on Institutional Cooperation (CIC), an association of nine midwestern states and two private universities, is an example of constructive interstate efforts on a voluntary nongovernment basis. The CIC has a number of significant achievements to its credit—such as the traveling scholar program, joint efforts in contracts abroad, and comparative studies in specific areas of university activity—but its most significant influence has come from its usefulness as a mechanism to initiate joint consultation among the members on a variety of subjects, such as library cooperation, articulation, new instructional programs, and new services.

On a broader scale, the work of the Education Commission of the States should be noted.[11] Also, the six regional accrediting bodies and the dozen or more agencies for accrediting of professional programs have encouraged planning at the institutional level. One stage in the accrediting procedure is the submission of an institutional self-evaluation report. To meet this requirement, the institution must undertake a comprehensive analysis of its mission, its priorities, its operations and personnel (both student and faculty), and its standards. The private philanthropic foundations have frequently followed the same procedure in making institutional grants as have some federal departments. In many instances, both for accreditation and for foundation or government grants, the institutions' self-evaluation reports are the first comprehensive surveys undertaken by the petitioners. Such reports have become a basis for continuing planning by the institutions.

Beyond the local, state, and regional efforts for improved planning, there has also been a search for common ground as a basis for federal assistance to higher education. The Education Facilities Act of 1963, whose provisions made possible the expansion of the physical plants nationwide, was an historic development of this kind, as was the enormous growth of federal participation in financing student aid through grants and loan funds. The Higher Education Amendments of 1972 marked out several other avenues of institutional aid but appropriations did not follow in the anticipated amounts. Further, divergencies within the higher education community, concerning the best way to provide broader federal assistance, prompted the Congress to authorize a study commission on the financing of postsecondary education in 1972. The commission's report brought national perspective to the objectives, problems, and issues; however, due to the differences in points of view and the complexity of factors involved, the report did not present any policy recommendations or a specific program for congressional action.

Although interinstitutional planning and coordination have grown markedly during the past two decades, there are many unresolved questions and problems to be faced, both by those who are involved in the administration of planning and by those who are responsible for evaluation of results. The general planning and coordination concept is widely accepted as a desirable development, but the very diversity of the mechanisms that have been established for that purpose reflect uncertainty as to the best method. Indeed, the only generalization possible now is that there is no one best way, no method which is uniformly applicable to all institutions or to all states or regions. Interinstitutional relations are affected by local experience, political climate, history, tradition, and leadership.

There are those who believe that the emphasis upon accountability, through quantitative evaluation of institutional performance, is an unfortunate development. They hold that the external agencies' intrusion into evaluation and planning is a threat to institutional autonomy and invites the politicization of institutional decisions. They believe the effort to measure the intangible outcomes of education—in benefits to the individual and to society—is unproductive, wasteful, and even futile. This attitude is reinforced by doubts concerning the worth or merit of new forms of program management that have become the tools of professional planners—systems analysis, program budgeting, cost-benefit ratios, and "policy analysis." The concern is well expressed by Martin Trow:[12]

> So I think that we must reexamine, and reexamine very critically, the assumption that the same kinds of public program assessments and reviews, using these new tools of rationalized management which seem so powerful when applied to highways, corrections, health care and welfare, are applicable, without fundamental rethinking and reformulation, to the systems and institutions of postsecondary education as well.

It seems clear, however, that regardless of doubts and reservations about coordination as the means to improve planning in higher education, the public context for higher education today — a time characterized as an era of "no-growth" and financial insecurity — will not allow a return to the former codes that governed the external relationships of colleges and universities. Administrative officers must face the inevitability of adversary relationships with coordinating boards, governors, legislatures, courts, and the federal government.[13] In addition to accrediting agencies, professional organizations, and others who presume to speak for the public — editors, commentators, and self-appointed spokesmen for university-related interest groups — the literature seems to say, according to K.P. Mortimer:[14]

> The combined impact of external pressures to be more accountable will push higher education closer to the status of a quasi-public utility. Executive agencies of government, including the federal government, the legislature (and Congress), and the courts will interject their conception of the public interest into decisions governing higher education.

In part, the agenda for planners in the next decade will concern cost regulations, managerial efficiency, codification of internal decision-making processes, behavioral accountability (the outcomes of learning, relevance of managerial technologies, and centralizing management while decentralizing educational functions.[15]

> In summary, the directions that pressure for accountability will take will be multiple and sometimes conflicting. There appears to be some inevitable tension between legitimate demands for accountability on the one hand and desires for institutional and individual autonomy on the other. The challenge of the next decade is to find a balance which assures both the protection of the public interest and of the educational environment so critical to effective scholarship, teaching and service.

The agenda for those who evaluate the performance of planners and coordinators will undoubtedly include the following fundamental questions raised by Martin Trow.[16]

> — Is increasing control over the forms and functions of higher education by central public agencies or authorities an inevitable concomitant of expansion and increased costs?

— Is the (increasing) role of public authorities presently a force working against diversity in higher education, in their functions and standards, their modes of governance, their forms of instruction, their sources of support and their relation to other institutions of society?

— If so, are these "standardizing" tendencies inherent in central governmental control, or is it possible for central governing and financing agencies to function in ways that sustain and increase the diversity in higher education? If so, what governing and funding structures would have that effect, and what principles of operation would govern their activities? How can efforts to support diversity be sustained against the political pressures arising out of (a) political and bureaucratic norms which prescribe equitable treatment of all comparable units and (b) growing egalitarian sentiments and policies?

— What are the conditions—the milieux and human relationships—which encourage creative intellectual, scholarly and scientific work in our colleges and universities? If, as I believe, those conditions are rare and fragile, how will they be affected by the broad structural, organizational, and political changes that we are witnessing? Should not a concern for the protection of the situations in which creative work of the highest quality is carried on by teachers and students be very high on our priorities?

As the pressures for expansion of higher education dominated the 1960s and led to increased interest in and support for interinstitutional planning and coordination, in the remaining decades of the twentieth century similar pressures will arise from increased demands for research and service during a time of financial stringency. Public concern with inflation, trends in living costs, high level of government expenditures, deficits, and high taxes, combined with a forecast of no-growth in the overall student population, will strengthen the expectation for increased planning and coordination. They will be even more important in a period of deceleration and retrenchment than in the preceding period of acceleration and expansion.

In the end, the goal of planning and coordination is to meet the pressure for change by design rather than improvisation, and by marshalling collective resources. Efforts to that end will surely increase.

Future Agenda

This sketch of the management of higher education in the United States, with an emphasis on the role of planning, reflects the diversity of the institutions as well as the complex interactions of the political, economic, and cultural conditions that comprise the environment for colleges and universities. It also reflects why national planning by the federal government is not likely to be accepted in the future. The traditional antipathy to federal control, with its risks of bureaucratic inefficiencies and homogenization of the institutions, works against the development of national planning as a policy objective.

Federal intrusion into the management of higher education may come piecemeal, however, through the administration of student financial assistance and support for categorical programs, and through enforcement of more general laws pertaining to such fields as health and occupational safety and civil rights. Often the quarrel on the issue of federal control is not rooted in the intent of Congress or in the legislation but in the restrictive and authoritarian regulations adopted by the administrative departments and agencies without consulting the institutions that are to be regulated. For example, when the states were directed to establish Educational Facilities Commissions (predecessors to "1202 Commissions") to formulate plans for the distribution of federal funds, the basic concept was accepted as a necessary premise for action. The administrative regulations implementing the law, however, were so restrictive and out of touch with operating realities that an aroused opposition forced their modification. In recent years, incidents of this kind have occurred with a frequency that reinforces the prevalent suspicion and fear of "federal control."

At the same time, the diverse mechanisms now operating at the state, interstate, and regional level, depend heavily on institutional participation and voluntary cooperation. They encourage governing boards and administrations to take a longer view of the goals and purposes of higher education and to more actively develop intramural planning that emphasizes productivity, efficiency, and cost and education effectiveness. Nearly all institutions accept the necessity to adapt to social change, recognize new conditions for operation, and continually seek improvement.

Higher education appreciates the importance of accountability. Certainly, improved planning will be of great assistance in dealing with the problems that inevitably arise in institutional relations. As enrollments level out and market demands for professional personnel change, a new emphasis on continuing planning will be a dominant characteristic of administration and management. Inflation and uncertainty of financial support will force institutions into new relationships with one another and with public agencies for coordination and external scrutiny.

The many sided nature of the social environment in which higher education operates ultimately creates the pressures for adjustment to change; it is the function of planning to anticipate that change. Structures and modes of operation must be evaluated in terms of how they serve the purpose of achieving greater effectiveness in a changing social setting. In considering the future of the management of higher education, one must therefore be aware of the larger issues to which higher education must respond.

Some of the unanswered questions that currently dominate professional discussion of the present and future performance of higher education are:

- As the unprecedented rate of the discovery of new knowledge and the corollary modification of the old continues to accelerate, how can research best be strengthened and extended?
- For the sound preparation of specialists in all fields of knowledge, how should institutions organize to respond effectively and promptly in curricular adjustments?
- The market for educated manpower fluctuates within relatively short periods. Forecasts of those fluctuations are notoriously undependable. How can the reliability of market information be improved to aid students in choosing a career and how can institutional resources be more appropriately utilized? How can market demands be more promptly and rationally related to the quantity and substance of professional educational programs? At the same time, how can the long-term social need for expertise be balanced against short-term market demand.
- How can institutions, through research and teaching, best contribute to problem solving in a context of ever-changing social concerns—for example, in such areas as conservation of natural resources, social justice, health

service, world hunger, and international relations?
- How should colleges and universities organize to serve new constituencies—adults, economically and culturally disadvantaged youth, professionals in need of continuing education—and do so in new ways and in new locations?
- What are the best ways to improve management efficiency and enhance productivity while preserving flexibility and creativity in operations and good morale in staff?
- Can liberal education, and the humane and intellectual values associated with it, be maintained as a core feature of a college education, reflected in student life and in faculty performance as well as in the curriculum?
- Will public financial assistance to students and institutions, at both state and federal levels, be adequate to make continued progress toward universal access to higher education?
- As educational opportunity is extended and services increased—to minority groups, to culturally disadvantaged individuals, to lower income families, to adults—how will the increased costs to institutions be met? All present sources of funding, private and public, will obviously be required and extended. Both public and independent institutions will need enlarged assistance from all sources.
- In the absence of quantitative measurements of or meaningful indices to the long-term benefits of higher education in the lives of people and to society, how can outcomes be interpreted to the public in ways that will satisfy the current demand for accountability and justify the increased financial support needed to sustain, improve, and extend institutional service?

The full and final answers to these questions and others will be rooted in public policies yet to be adopted. They are beyond the reach of institutional planning. However, although they do not determine the answers, institutions of higher education can identify the issues and clarify the debate by providing relevant information and analysis formulated in terms of the public interest rather than the welfare of institutions *per se*. Further, they can move to change that which is within their power and aggressively interpret their positions on aspects of public policy that require external action. In the search for answers, many variables that cannot be anticipated now will also be influential. Unforeseen climactic events will affect the course of the nation, and with it the course of higher education. What will be the parallels to past wars and depressions, to the creation of radio and television, to atomic energy, to the moon shots and space exploration, to street riots, to student disruption, to the shifts and turns of political leadership? These will be the variables in an unpredictable future.[17]

> But the constants are there, too. New knowledge and advanced learning are essential to a civilized society, regardless of the variables. As long as the technological society exists, the centrality of higher education will remain. Further, as attention is turned increasingly to the creation and expansion of human services within society, higher education will be called upon to train those who staff the service components. Optimism derived from these constants is more than the residue of an old-fashioned faith. It is a realistic acknowledgment of where we are, and it can be grounds for confidence despite the variables.

As we grapple with unknowns, the future promises difficulty, as it always has, but it will not be bleak if goals and actions are aligned with social benefits and if the members of the professional academy have the will, sense of mission, and imagination to meet opposition, competition for public attention, and changing demands and expectations. Sound planning will be essential in this endeavor.

FOOTNOTES

1. J.V. Baldridge, D.V. Curtis, G. Ecker, and G.L. Riley, "Diversity in Higher Education," *The Journal of Higher Education*, Vol. XLVIII, No. 4 (July/August 1977), p. 368.
2. The Association of Governing Boards (a national organization devoted to presenting national perspectives on higher education and counsel and advice in board procedures and practices) now has over 1,250 institutional members.
3. Carnegie Foundation for the Advancement of Teaching, *More Than Survival* (San Francisco: Jossey-Bass Publishers, 1976), pp. 85-91.
4. E.C. Lee and F.M. Bowen, *Managing Multicampus Systems*. Report for the Carnegie Council on Policy Studies in Higher Education (San Francisco: Jossey-Bass Publishers, 1975).

5. D.D. Henry, *Challenges Past, Challenges Present.* Essay for the Carnegie Council on Policy Studies in Higher Education (San Francisco: Jossey-Bass Publishers, 1975), p. 18.
6. President's Committee on Education Beyond the High School, *Second Report to the President* (Washington, D.C.: U.S. Government Printing Office, 1957), pp. 16-17.
7. *Ibid.,* p. 59.
8. *Ibid.,* p. 60.
9. The 1202 Commissions were authorized under a 1972 Amendment to the Higher Education Act of 1965.
10. Carnegie Foundation for the Advancement of Teaching, *The States and Higher Education* (San Francisco: Jossey-Bass Publishers, 1976), p. 17.
11. Education Commission of the States, Annual Report, *1977 New Directions* (Denver, Colorado: ECS, 1977).
12. Martin Trow, "The Public Lives of Higher Education," Paper presented at the Second National Forum on New Planning and Management Practices in Post-Secondary Education, sponsored by the Education Commission of the States, Chicago, November 16, 1973 (p. 16).
13. A case in point is the eruption of a major controversy between the institutions and the Veterans Administration. In order to prevent what it regards as abuses of the provisions of the "G.I. Bill," the V.A. has moved to specify policy as to what constitutes a satisfactory rate of progress toward a degree, the validity of nondegree programs, attendance requirements in residence courses, and similar matters ordinarily left to institutional administration. As a result, twenty-seven lawsuits have been filed in twenty states (*New York Times,* July 13, 1977).
14. K.P. Mortimer, *Accountability in Higher Education* (Washington, D.C.: National Academy of Sciences, 1974), p. 47.
15. *Ibid.,* p. 50.
16. Trow, *op. cit.,* pp. 28-29.
17. Henry, *op. cit.,* pp. 159-60.

REFERENCES

BALDRIDGE, J.V., CURTIS, D.V., ECKER, G., AND RILEY, G.L. "Diversity in Higher Education." *The Journal of Higher Education.* Vol. XLVIII, No. 4 (July/August, 1977), pp. 367-388.

BENDER, L.W. *Federal Regulation and Higher Education.* Washington, D.C.: The American Association for Higher Education, 1977.

CARNEGIE FOUNDATION FOR THE ADVANCEMENT OF TEACHING. *More Than Survival.* San Francisco: Jossey-Bass Publishers, 1976.

CARNEGIE FOUNDATION FOR THE ADVANCEMENT OF TEACHING. *The States and Higher Education.* San Francisco: Jossey-Bass Publishers, 1975.

EDUCATION COMMISSION OF THE STATES. Annual Report, *1977 New Directions.* Denver, Colorado: ECS, 1977.

HENRY, D.D. *Challenges Past, Challenges Present.* Essay for the Carnegie Council on Policy Studies in Higher Education. San Francisco: Jossey-Bass Publishers, 1975.

LEE, E.C., BOWEN, F.M. *Managing Multicampus Systems.* Report for the Carnegie Council on Policy Studies in Higher Education. San Francisco: Jossey-Bass Publishers, 1975.

MORTIMER, K.P. *Accountability in Higher Education.* Washington, D.C.: American Association for Higher Education, 1972.

NATIONAL BOARD ON GRADUATE EDUCATION. *Federal Policy Alternatives Toward Graduate Education.* Washington, D.C.: National Academy of Sciences, January, 1974.

NATIONAL COMMISSION ON THE FINANCING OF POSTSECONDARY EDUCATION. *Financing Postsecondary Education in the United States.* Washington, D.C.: U.S. Government Printing Office, 1973.

PRESIDENT'S COMMISSION ON HIGHER EDUCATION. *Higher Education for American Democracy,* Volumes 1-6. New York: Harper & Row, 1947.

PRESIDENT'S COMMITTEE ON EDUCATION BEYOND THE HIGH SCHOOL. Second Report to the President, Washington, D.C.: U.S. Government Printing Office, 1957.

TROW, M. "The Public and Private Lives of Higher Education." Paper read at the Second National Forum on New Planning and Management Practices in Post-Secondary Education, sponsored by the Education Commission of the States, Chicago, November 16, 1973.

COMMISSION ON FINANCING HIGHER EDUCATION. *Final Report: Nature and Needs of Higher Education.* New York: Columbia University Press 1952.

EFFECTIVENESS OF THE SYSTEM
LYMAN A. GLENNY

Introduction

Since their early days, colleges and universities contributed to the well-being of both the individual and society. The relationship of education to the welfare of the individual emphasizes the subtle, intangible elements which contribute to personal satisfaction and happiness, greater equity in self-esteem, and to mobility among the classes in democratic societies. The full potential for human development through education may never be clearly known nor, if known, fully implemented. The same conclusion may be drawn with respect to the contribution of education to societal goals. The numerous desired outcomes sought by competing groups may never be identified, and if identified, not attempted or not achieved by the educational system.

Goals and aspirations of the imaginative human mind will always exceed the capacity for implementation by an organized educational system. For society as a whole, inventive humans seek so many divergent or diametrically opposed sets of values that no educational system, however willing, well financed, or staffed could ever fill any but a small fraction of them. Society needs persons who are productive economically, good citizens, cooperative, and self-sacrificing, even while groups or individuals may seek private objectives at high variance with those of the society as a whole. Individual self-fulfillment may, as Aristotle and certain eighteenth-century theorists claimed, be achieved only as a fully participating member of society. The penalty recommended and often imposed for those failing to seek such self-fulfillment was, to use a phrase coined many centuries later, to send them to Coventry-osterization.

Today in democratic societies, the goals of higher education can be agreed to in principle, if broadly enough stated, but become matters of diverse individual opinion as the objectives become more precise or instrumental. Hence, when tendering goals and objectives, modern higher educational systems use terms so general and so broad that both the person with particularized objectives and society with its need for skilled manpower and increased productivity find agreement in them. In evaluating the effectiveness of the higher education system one must be aware that to conclude that a system is effective may gloss myriad individual and group ideas of what ought to be but is not.

This section is a modest attempt to evaluate the social effectiveness of the United States system of higher education. Other sections focus on management, efficiency, and coordination of the many systems. Discussion of each subject attempts to show the degree to which certain broad goals have been achieved. One may ask the old question, "Whose goals?" The perspective may vary considerably if one is from the upper middle class or from a working class family, or if one is from a minority group or a student, a government official or an industrial employer. One man's goals may be another man's anathema.

Heterogeneity in viewpoints increases as evaluations made within a system are compared to those of outsiders. Almost all evaluations by insiders show positive results while almost all evaluations by outsiders, that is, lay persons, politicians, and influential business people, fall toward the negative side. This is especially true of education. According to a national 1969 survey completed at the height of student disruptions on campus, 85 percent of the students were satisfied with their education, while 90 percent of the faculty were satisfied with their jobs.

We employed several dimensions as bases for evaluating effectiveness. We examined the major problem areas which the nation directly or indirectly assigns to higher education for solution. At least one goal of higher education is to aid in solving social, economic and manpower problems, certainly a view contrary to that of Thorsten Veblen and of the late Robert Hutchins, both of whom valued education for its own sake and for individual development and gratification, not for solving practical everyday problems. We also assume that higher institutions and their faculties will raise the critical issues which relate to the society, clarifying them, indicating direction and possible ways of resolving them. This function of criticism seems never to have been assigned specifically to any university by a government but has nonetheless been assumed as a fundamental role for universities throughout the democratic world. Finally, we reviewed many sets of evaluative criteria developed by others for the specialized areas with which higher education deals and for general, expected, social outcomes. The Carnegie Commission, the National Commissions on Financing Postsecondary Education, the Berkeley Center for Research and Development in Higher Education, the Association of Governing Boards, and many individuals—such as Callan on state coordinating boards, Paltridge on governing boards, Barak and Berdahl on program reviews, Medsker on nontraditional programs, and Hodgkinson on innovative and developing colleges—provide analyses or lists of evaluation criteria along with means for application.

Different sets of criteria may be developed by each new commission or task force in assessing the effectiveness of higher education at state and national levels. The criteria adopted fit the predilections of commission members in keeping with the particular emphasis of their studies. After reviewing many of these criteria, we distilled eight areas which appear appropriate to use in this evaluation of the social impact of the United States system. In addition, we drew heavily from criteria developed by the Center for Research and Development in Higher Education at Berkeley on effectiveness of budgeting, planning, and coordinating higher education.

Each criterion is applied to broad developments across the nation and to specific gains and deficiencies in each area. In discussing current developments and trends, we will also speculate about future prospects and implications.

Social Purposes

The eight criteria selected to assess the social effectiveness of the system of higher education are: educational diversity; access; priorities; flexibility, innovation, and change; extending knowledge and research; cultural contributions; other contributed results; and excellence and quality. These categories, rather broad and all encompassing, tend to overlap; none is mutually exclusive, either in terms of its characteristics or in terms of the trends that affect it.

Educational Diversity

In a preceding section of this study, John Shea discussed the tremendous diversity of institutions which comprise higher education and postsecondary education in this nation. Most of this diversity derives from fortuitous events and microplanning rather than from macrostate or national planning. (The federal-state land grant movement could be considered an exception.) As the great variety of institutions ranges from highly specialized professional schools to two-year community colleges, to four-year liberal arts colleges (mostly private), to comprehensive colleges (mostly public), to large universities (public and private), and a few elitist institutions—so, too, the student bodies vary in each type of institution.

In most of the over 3,000 institutions of higher education recognized by the U.S. Office of Education, one may find a broad range of student talents and abilities but they usually cluster around some standard which represents the core profile of the student body. Even the single university with several different campuses finds that a somewhat different type of student is attracted to each different campus. For example, student profiles vary rather widely among the various campuses of the University of California. Although by law the University of California only accepts students who have graduated in the upper 12.5 percent of their high school classes, the social, political, economic, and religious attitudes and values of students account for the differences in student-institutional profiles. A student entering one campus may find a fairly alien environment while another campus in the same university may be a haven for that student. The range of diversity of institutions seems to have grown out of the felt needs of certain types of students. Hence, individual institutions cater to and can accomodate some types of students more successfully than others. The happy diversity of American higher education and easy transfer and mobility allow for this, particularly at undergraduate levels.

Are the results of education from these wide-ranging institutions alike or different in terms of the degrees awarded and the prestige attached to them? As in the rest of the world, some institutions have attained a degree of prestige unobtainable by the vast majority of the others—even though other institutions may have been in existence as long as those that have acquired prestige. Even during the great expansion and fairly liberal funding of the 1950s and 1960s, few new or old institutions were able to pull themselves up to the level of the elite. Many, however, changed their roles and missions by developing from two- to four-year colleges, and then later to comprehensive state colleges, and perhaps a bit later to an "emerging university," but few made it to the elite group however much that remained the model for emulation.

Yet, whatever the reputation or quality, particular types of institutions offer similar kinds of degrees: two-year colleges award associate degrees and certain technical certificates; four-year colleges offer the bachelor's degree; five-year universities confer both bachelor's and master's degrees; and the large universities offer doctorates as well as B.A. and M.A. degrees. The currency of the degrees in the market place often reflects the prestige of the institution. During the latter part of the 1960s and early seventies this distinction seemed to have faded a little but as standards are tightened in the later seventies, the "old school tie" syndrome seems to be reinforced. Certainly, the elite institutions have suffered few enrollment drops however much enrollment may have declined in less pretigious schools. State colleges and comprehensive public colleges appear most vulnerable to enrollment reductions. Community colleges are holding better and rank next to the elite group because of their many technical courses and emphasis on manpower training...or at least education for job entry. It would appear that the prestigious private colleges and the large research-oriented universities draw from the upper ability percentiles of elgible students while the community colleges try to maintain their enrollments by responsiveness to immediate community goals and general manpower needs, drawing from the full range of student aptitude and interest.

The spectrum of institutional types reflects society's and students' needs, so do the ranges of programs at the individual campus or system level. The number of specialized professional and disciplinary areas for which degrees are offered may range from a handful in the small liberal arts college or community college on up to hundreds in the large research universities. Within these universities an ever developing recombination of disciplines along with newly discovered knowledge continuously broadens the amount of diversity while ensuring that courses will be *au courant*. Within a college or university, one may enroll in programs leading to a career in auto mechanics, electronics, computer programming, biophysics research, atomic chemistry, or ancient Chinese art forms. The opportunities for each specialization depend on the aptitude and interests of the students and on the accessibility of a particular institution.

Postsecondary schools other than those considered to be higher education may be operated as profit-making businesses, by industry, by labor unions, and by a host of social and religious organizations. Among other factors, the development of these alternative opportunities has taken the enrollment pressure off higher institutions; the proportion of high school graduates going on to the colleges and universities has dropped from its 1968 high.

Some states—such as New York, Illinois, California, and Pennsylvania—have the full range of programs and types of institutions while other states with less industry and fewer people may offer a much narrower range of educational opportunities. Diversity of programs stands as one of the major strengths of higher education in the United States. This diversity, however, may not be available to all who seek it. A recognized problem on which the states and the federal government continue to work is that of obtaining equal access to alternative programs for lower income and less prepared students.

Access

The Bakke case now before the U.S. Supreme Court concerns the use of racial quotas in admitting students. The plaintiff contends that quotas violated the Bill of Rights (more particularly the Fourteenth Amendment) of the United States Constitution by denying equal protection. No case in twenty-five years illustrates more clearly the intent of the higher education system to equalize and make up for deficiencies in the proportion of minority students admitted to the system. Nor does any case more clearly show the difficulty the system confronts in trying to achieve a generally accepted social goal. Providing a quota or number of places for a disadvantaged group seemed a sure way of correcting this deficiency but it also appears to deny to other students, not of the minority group, the right to enter a program even though they may have superior qualifications. A decision declaring quotas unconstitutional would surprise few legal scholars, for the Court has long held that racial quotas for any purpose clearly conflict with the Constitution. The Court may allow other criteria which would accomplish the same ends. The Court will not disagree with the social goal but with the illegal means of obtaining it; a mere procedural matter some would say.

Procedural devices, however, lie at the heart of most access problems. Tests used to measure knowledge and capability are procedural devices and they too are faulty and attacked by minority spokespersons for their cultural bias and discriminatory outcomes. As a consequence, tests have been dropped as screening devices or used only in conjunction with other criteria for admission to some colleges and universities. Nevertheless, the elite liberal arts colleges and prestigious universities have found ways of keeping out all but the very brightest of students.

But to block a student from entry to one institution or program may not prevent his or her access to one or a dozen others of similar kind. The evidence on access shows that the United States has made more places available to a larger proportion of the traditional college-age population—eighteen to twenty-two years old—than any nation in the world. At one point during 1968-69 over half of the high school graduates and over 40 percent of the age group entered a college or university, while over seventeen million others enrolled in some adult form of postsecondary education. As a result of ad hoc planning and rapid training of thousands of faculty members, the system as a whole (but not each institution) was able to accommodate nearly every student who actually applied during the 1960s—an enviable record for the nation which seemed to believe that every young person required college experience. During the past ten years that assumption no longer holds, with many young people choose alternative postsecondary opportunities or foregoing college for a number of years in favor of travel or work. Students discovered that the difference in income between those with college degrees and those with high school diplomas is decreasing rapidly as a greater proportion of the total workforce has college degrees, and as the former ease of obtaining a position gives way to taking jobs of lesser status and lesser pay. Despite this changed attitude, particularly by white males, if minorities and women are to succeed in upward social and economic mobility, the college degree becomes an essential wedge for opening opportunities. Access continues to be of concern to this minority population and hence to the government whose financial capabilities and nondiscriminatory policies can facilitate such entry.

State and local governments provided the major funding toward building or expanding colleges and universities, making greater access possible. The community colleges have played an especially significant role in meeting this need, although all types of institutions have sought to provide access. The vast majority of all places in higher education have been furnished by state and local governments.

The federal government more assertively than the states has insisted on policies that would prevent discrimination in the admission of students. The antidiscrimination legislation, based on the "equal protection" clause in the Fourteenth Amendment, prohibits state governments as well as institutions and individuals from preventing entry to higher institutions for reasons of sex or race. Elaborate reporting mechanisms require colleges and universities, public and private, to show how positive action is taken to prevent discrimination and to encourage the admission of women and minorities. Some states have also passed antidiscrimination legislation and statutes which provide for affirmative action in relation to access of low-income, minority, and female populations. These laws occasionally go beyond the federal statutes by requiring stricter compliance by the colleges and universities.

Federal direct aid to students has increased greatly in the past few years, going from $2 billion in 1970 to $4 billion in 1977.[1] More funds have been provided to aid the students directly through grants, work-study programs, and guaranteed loans. Most of the grant and work-study money goes to low-income students who show the most financial need; while most loans are taken up by middle and even upper income students.

The great majority of the states have also instituted similar kinds of financial aid programs for students, often directed at the same populations as the federal programs. The amount of state student-aid funds has also increased dramatically, from $269 million in 1972 to $1.1 billion in 1977.[2]

The results of actions by both the federal and state governments show that objectives are being achieved. The proportion of women in the college age-group and the percentage of women in college have risen gradually until in 1977 the number of women exceeded the number of men enrolled. (In part this phenomenon can be explained by the drop in the proportion of white males attending college.) The proportion of eighteen to thirty-four year old blacks in college also rose substantially. The National Center for Educational Statistics reports that between 1970 and 1975, in four regions in the United States, enrollments of whites in college ranged from 12 to 18 percent of the population subgroup though for any one region enrollment patterns have not changed by more than 1 percent since 1970. In contrast, the enrollments of blacks rose in each region. In the Northeast, the increase was especially dramatic, rising from 8.8 percent in 1970 to 16.8 in 1975. The increases in other regions were: 2.5 percentage points in the Southeast, 7.2 points in the Central region, and 4.8 in the West. In the Central and Northeast regions, the proportion of white and black age-groups in college is approximately the same. The National Longitudinal Study of the U.S. Office of Education shows that blacks from the 1972 high school graduating class surpassed their white classmates in their persistence in some form of schooling two years later: "For virtually every ability and socioeconomic status group, the blacks in the study were showing greater staying [persistence] power than whites."[3] The proportion of blacks eighteen to twenty-four years old enrolled in college increased from 7.4 percent in 1967 to 13.2 percent in 1977. It must be added, however, that a disproportionate share of the black population attends community colleges in comparison to whites, who disproportionately attend four-year colleges and universities.

While higher education enrolled 11.2 million persons in 1975-76, the remainder of formally recognized postsecondary schools served 17.3 million students. The courses and programs of these postsecondary schools often compete directly with those in nearby colleges (especially community colleges) by offering languages, cosmetology, business, technical, trade, and correspondence work. Again, both the diversity and access to postsecondary education are greatly augmented through these alternatives.

However, despite all the diversity, all the student aid programs, and all the policy effort to equalize opportunity at the postsecondary and collegiate level, the United States still faces several major problems. First, the proportion of young people entering college from families in the high-income brackets continues to exceed by four or five times that of students from the lower socioeconomic levels. This condition is slowly improving but the disparity remains very marked. Early childhood development, lack of motivation, and other socio-psychological conditions appear to account for much of the difference. The special programs of the federal government to overcome these differences have not yet shown dramatic improvements.

The second problem concerns the change occurring in the proportion of young people who graduate from high schools. Historically, in Europe tracking in the secondary schools accounted in large part for the lower college enrollment rates. In part the lower proportion of high school graduates also explains the enrollment rate in the United States. The National Center for Educational Statistics (NCES) reports that in 1967 high school graduates comprised 76.5 percent of the seventeen-year old population. By 1975, that figure had dropped to 74.4 percent.[4]

The third problem results in part from the reduced percentage of high school graduates and from the lower proportion of high school graduates who enter college the following Fall term. In 1976, enrollments were actually less than the year before, although the number of high school graduates increased by about 60,000. The age cohort, eighteen to twenty-two years old, will continue to increase until 1980 while college enrollments are leveling off. The factors which are thought to be contributing to this significant change are: an oversupply of some types of manpower, a general unemployment rate of about 7 percent, a disillusionment with higher education on the part of public officials, and the tendency of the incomes of those with and without college degrees to converge.

Delays in entrance to college may also account for part of this trend. Because of the great increase in the average age of persons in collegiate institutions, the U.S. Census Bureau and NCES report data not only for the eighteen to twenty-four year old age group but also for the twenty-five to thirty-four year old age group. Counting the total population of eighteen to thirty-four year olds, the proportion of that age group going to college increased from 25.8 percent in 1970 to 26.2 percent in 1975.[5]

Social Priorities

The base of social needs determines the amount of encouragement for access and for providing a diversity of programs and institutions. Increasingly complex problems resulting from urbanization, industrialization, and technological development require talented, well trained, and well educated citizens. In the following section, the effectiveness of the higher educational system in meeting manpower needs, solving major social and technical problems, and in providing social services will be briefly evaluated.

Manpower

Since 1956, concern for the training of skilled manpower for technical and professional positions has tended to dominate federal, state, and local policy in funding higher education programs. Other educational programs—general education and the liberal arts, the major focus of higher education for most of the century from 1840-1940 gave way to an almost exclusive concern for manpower training to improve the efficiency and productivity of the economy.

The success of this emphasis on college education for meeting manpower and other social needs is best illustrated by the increases in the various levels of degrees awarded, especially graduate and professional. In 1961-62, 388,000 bachelor's degrees were awarded in the United States; by 1975-76, this figure had increased to 909,000. During the same time period, the proportion of twenty-two year olds receiving degrees increased from 20.2 percent to 24.8 percent. About 25 percent of the twenty-two year old population is projected to receive degrees until 1980—that is, the same proportion as at the present time. The number of master's degrees rose from about 78,000 in 1960 to 316,000 in 1976, an increase of 313 percent. Doctoral degrees were awarded to 9,800 students in 1960 and to 35,000 in 1976—or a 267 percent increase. The projection for 1979-80 is for 382,000 master's and 36,000 doctor's degrees to be awarded.

This increase in the number of degrees awarded grew out of governmental efforts to increase diversity and access to higher education; first in the late 1940s by the G.I. Bill, which funded thousands of veterans of World War II; later in the mid-fifties when the federal government heavily funded the expansion of places for the hard sciences and mathematics in reaction to Sputnik; concurrently by both state and federal governments in building new colleges and universities, also resulting in the vast expansion of the community college system; and most recently, in providing massive funding of direct aid to students.

Student demand as opposed to manpower planning primarily

shaped these developments; this has traditionally been the case in the United States. From the post-World War II period to the late 1960s, society expected that all young people should have some college education. But during the latter part of the sixties, the job market tightened, federal expenditures for research and development curtailed sharply, and the long-term shortage of elementary and secondary school teachers finally ended. As the number of persons graduating from college continued to increase and the economic situation continued to deteriorate in the early 1970s, employment prospects for all college graduates were adversely affected. Moreover, another fifteen million college graduates were expected to enter the labor force between 1975 and 1985—about 800,000 more than the number of projected job openings.

Some policy makers call into question the surplus of manpower which student demand produces and ask for more manpower need studies and greater accuracy in forecasting manpower requirements. However, in a democratic, pluralistic society, complexity almost prohibits even rough estimates of manpower needs. The task tends to defy human comprehension of ascertaining the plans or intents of individual enterprises or services to expand or contract—the difficulty in placing roughly projected needs into the thousands of job classifications, the effects of federal government policies in foreign relations, health, welfare, education, energy, and other forms of social services, and the impact of the policies of the fifty state governments. For the immediate future in the United States the student demand model is very likely to continue, even though it may bring about a "surplus" of certain specialists while producing too few in other areas.

Higher education responds in a flexible manner to shifts in manpower demands even though manpower forecasting is a quite inexact science. Federal intervention to produce particular manpower after Sputnik led to expenditures of $5 billion a year for research and development; but with the impending surplus, the federal government dropped its support to $2 billion a year, resulting in drastic revisions in curriculum planning by institutions along with substantial reallocations of funds. In general, however, the state and federal governments have avoided intervening in curricular development to change manpower supplies; rather they have relied on the institutions to respond to students who presumably assess the job market before they select their major course of study. The fact that students do shift majors and that institutions respond is evident in data on enrollment shifts during the last dozen years. The U.S. Census Bureau reports that during the period 1966-1974 vast changes took place in enrollments among college disciplines. For example, emrollments in the physical sciences dropped by more than 40 percent and those in mathematics and statistics by almost 30 percent; enrollments in engineering decreased by 23 percent. During the same eight-year period, enrollments in the biological health sciences increased by 33 percent, in forestry and agriculture by 42 percent, and in the social sciences by 20 percent.

In a shorter time period, between 1972-1974, enrollment sometimes shifted in directions opposite to the trends of the entire eight-year period. For example, in those two years, engineering enrollments went up almost 15 percent (as opposed to the decline of 23 percent in the eight-year period), while social science enrollments dropped by 19 percent against the increase of 20 percent in the eight years.[6] These remarkable adjustments to changes in demand provide support for the assumption that higher education can be responsive to a dynamic and fluctuating labor market.

Indeed the responsiveness of the system has led to surpluses in a great many fields of study if one measures degree output against positions which have traditionally been filled by such degree holders. This was a predictable outcome, for the U.S. Department of Labor has been indicating for over fifteen years that only 20 percent of the positions in the total work force require a college education, and will until the year 2000. For most other positions, a high school education followed by short courses of on-the-job training apparently constitute sufficient work preparation. Nevertheless, the number of graduates now exceeds the immediate demand at every degree level, so that the ratio of graduates to the number of jobs increases steadily. The result forces graduates into lower level occupations formerly held by persons without college training. The graduate has a job, but it is not at the level aspired to when taking the degree. At the same time, persons without degrees are forced into still lower status jobs and those, in turn, replace others. This phenomenon can be likened to that of the 1920s when the high school diploma became the minimum standard for many positions which formerly required only a few years of education or simply required basic literacy.

Surpluses in many occupational specializations will probably be with us for another ten years or more. After that, shortages may appear because the number of young people of college age will be declining about 23 percent from 1980 until the mid-1990s. The drop in the college-enrollment rate reflects manpower factors to some degree, but students continue to attend college and to take programs which appear unrealistic in terms of job placement for many of them.[7] Astin survey date on 1976 freshmen show that over 50 percent of them expect to be in occupations which call for at least a bachelor's degree;[8] yet the job market currently requires only 20 percent of the labor force to have a college degree. Bachelor's degrees are currently awarded to 23 percent of the total population of twenty-year olds and, of course, other students are receiving master's and doctorate degrees in the same year.

Higher education can be said to meet the needs of the society for trained manpower, although unevenly at times. It does appear, however, that women have less chance for success in the job market than men do. In 1977, job opportunities for all college graduates increased 77 percent, but women accounted for only one-fourth of those positions. Some career counselors attribute this situation to the fact that many women major in fields where job offers are less plentiful—teaching, the humanities, social science—rather than engineering, accounting, and the sciences. Hence, in spite of successful affirmative action by the colleges and universities to enroll women students, women tend to become the "surplus" graduates rather than the needed ones.

Social Problem Solving

Industrial societies expect higher education to supply university and college graduates to solve the many social problems which plague urbanized areas and the technocratic society. This expectation has recent origins in the United States. Prior to World War I, little more than the training of ministers, lawyers, and gentlemen (and a few gentlewomen) was anticipated as an outcome of college education. But as research and science became university functions, the government depended more heavily on the expert knowledge of professors to help solve governmental problems. During World War I there was an increasing use of university resources in the organization and conduct of the war effort, while in the 1920s the land grant universities expanded services to a largely rural and farming population through agricultural extension and experiment programs. The state university, especially in the Midwest and West, became a service agency for government by responding to its politically determined social priorities. The programs to fight the Great Depression of the 1930s were almost exclusively developed by persons drawn directly from the great research universities of the nation. By World War II, higher education not only responded to the technological requirements for weapons, clothing, transportation, rationing, and controlling distribution systems, it also trained thousands of officers, technicians, and scientists for employment by the armed forces. But the Russians' orbiting of Sputnik created the greatest single demand by government on the colleges and universities. The billions of dollars poured into the space program by the federal government—to step up research and knowledge and the production of scientists, engineers, and mathematicians—resulted in the most extensive transformation within collegiate institutions of any government action prior to that time. Federal largess was more than matched by state efforts to keep up with the tremendous increase in the numbers of persons who sought a college education. Education began to be looked upon as a panacea for all social and economic problems of the society. Young people were expected to go to college, for their own welfare and that of the country. Manpower production for beating the Russians to the moon turned out so successfully that many persons began to believe that all social problems might be solved in the same way...through university research and manpower production.

By the late 1960s, both as a result of the revolt of young people against "technocracy" and the assumed problems which it entailed and against the sciences for supporting the war in Vietnam, students began to shift away from the hard sciences into the social and biological sciences. Part of the new emphasis can be laid to the dimishment of federal funding of the space program and the related decrease in research and training in the universities. More important were the aspirations of young people to solve such social problems as slum clearance, housing, health care, transportation, and environment deficiences—air, water, and open land. Economics, public policy, political science, and psychology became the popular programs for students who rapidly drifted away from the hard sciences and engineering. It took only a few years of experience with the new domestic programs for policy makers to realize that the state of knowledge for solving social problems—as opposed to purely technological ones—remained far behind. However, as disillusionment set in, rather than pouring vast resources into social science research, the federal government adopted a laissez faire approach to higher education while inaugurating one new social action program after another, few of which obtained their ostensible objectives.

Nevertheless, the quality of life, the longevity of the human being, and the standard of living for the vast majority of Americans improved greatly during the past twenty years, and much, if not most, of these outcomes can be attributed to the knowledge and expertise produced by the colleges and universities. We do have cleaner air, clearer water, more nationally protected forests and wild places, and more slum clearance. We also have increased life expectancy sharply in the past few years by a rapid decline in the death rate, from 38.2 per 1,000 in 1960 to 31.9 in 1975. We cannot, on the other hand, overlook the negative aspects—that slums still exist in many cities, poor housing is common, the care of the aged dismal, women and minorities fail to achieve much upward mobility, and new suburbs continue to take much of the richest, most productive agricultural land.

Yet technology, the product of higher education and research, has been at the heart of the improvements that have been made and it is the university trained expert that makes possible the vast highways and air transport systems, the telephone, radio, and television communication networks, the standards for improving safety in factories, building construction, and mining, the computers which are used for much of the accounting, record-keeping and mathematical computations of the society, and the improvements in food production, preservation, and delivery. Every advancement cannot be directly attributed to higher institutions. Independent research agencies, governmental, and industrial laboratories play major roles too; however, the persons performing these functions in other than university settings are trained and educated in the colleges and universities of the nation.

University and College Services

In addition to the general provisions of manpower and knowledge for use by other organizations, the universities and colleges provide services for a great variety of constituent groups. The phenomenon of the new modern, scientific and computer industries clustering around one or more universities is widespread in the country. These organizations draw on the faculties and the research conducted within the university walls. Small retail and wholesale businesses receive managerial and marketing advice from college institutes created expressly for such purposes.

Thousands of faculty members serve on advisory committees which relate to almost every service that governments, federal, state and local, perform for the people. Other thousands provide consulting services to governments, industry, and business. In agriculture the universities improve the quality, size and variety of fruits, vegetables, and grains in addition to inventing new procedures for processing and preserving these products. The Agricultural Extension Service and the Agricultural Experiment Stations of the land grant universities have been the primary instruments shaping the farming practices and the kinds of products raised. The historical record of these colleges provides the model by which other college and university institutes and centers guide activities to other aspects of American life.

Foreign governments and industries too draw heavily from the American college and university for similar kinds of service. Contracts with institutions in this country and with individual faculty members provide for everything from the creating of an entirely new university to improving irrigation methods, to the fabricating of metal products.

The very diversity of higher education makes possible the myriad service activities which cover the gamut of economic and social services. This service orientation, "the state is our campus," has made higher education an integral part of government and its economic and social life. The public demands for an ever increasing number of such services reveals the worth the citizens see in the higher educational system.

Flexibility, Innovation, and Change

The charge is often made that faculties and institutions conserve rather than change or innovate. Perhaps, as is the case for faculties in Europe and elsewhere, the amount of time and costs each faculty member has invested in his or her area of specialization makes it uncomfortable or unprofitable to change. Much evidence supports the view that faculties adhere to the status quo more than administrators do, and administrators more than students. Some critics further argue that major changes in institutional mission and function occur only as a result of outside pressure, rarely from forces within. Yet change, innovation, and new missions have made entirely new types of institutions out of existing ones or have, at least, significantly modified programs and student composition.

The evidence cited in preceding pages—that the physical sciences have dropped 40 percent in enrollment in an eight-year period while biological health sciences increased 33 percent—gives some indication that change does occur in program emphasis within institutions. These figures represent averages; hence the individual institutions in some cases have had much more drastic shifts in program enrollment. These modifications, possibly as much as any other single factor, show the flexibility of higher institutions. Ironically enough, neither planning nor strong leadership—the research-based hallmark qualities of effective change—were necessary to make these adaptations. Rather, student-faculty ratios were reduced in some program areas and increased in others by routine means; new faculty members were hired in the expanding areas while none were hired for retirements or resignations in the declining enrollment areas. The machinery of normal good management provided the means for these large and important shifts in program emphasis to occur. The very character of some institutions changed as a result. Even the governments were not strongly importuned to supply additional funding in order to make these program transitions more easily accomplished without dislocation of existing resources. They will change again if similar shifts in the opposite or divergent directions should occur. Yet changes of this kind, however important they are, do not represent innovation but mere change. A faculty senate or institutional planning body probably could not accomplish similar magnitudes of change by planning and persuasion.

The great innovations in colleges and universities have resulted from either strong aggressive leadership from within or a great deal of pressure by policy bodies from without...sometimes by persuasive use of money grants. The research on innovation by Medsker and others shows rather clearly that the innovator tends to be young, nontenured, not influential within inner faculty circles and more inclined to student welfare than to faculty politics. Without the full active support from one or more of the top administrators, especially the president, an innovative program has little chance of approval for experimentation and even less for long-term commitment of funding.

Leadership for internal redirection has not been widespred, although notable exceptions can be found. In almost every case, finance and/or enrollment problems create the need to display strength in leading the institution in new directions by cutting existing programs and inaugurating new ones. Internal change has rarely been sought for purely educational reasons except for the addition of entirely new graduate programs (of which 1,968 have been initiated in the past six years).

Rather, major educational innovations usually come through policy pressure exerted by legislatures or through the availability of outside funds sufficient to get an innovation underway for a year or two. Legislators and governors sometimes reserve funds at the central state level—usually with the state coordinating board as in Illinois—for competition among the institutions in developing innovations in program, delivery systems, or in the organization of curricula. These funds, while not large, have drawn significant institutional competition for a share—and for the types of programs intended by the state. States also assume the costs of entirely new programs presented for approval by the institutions during the annual budget cycle (such as the graduate programs noted earlier). The process for approval of such programs—first through the internal machinery of the institution and then through the state coordinating board, the executive budget office, and finally the legislature and its staffs—makes it hazardous for all but the most justifiable and quite possibly the most prosaic of them. State governments support the new university-without-walls concept, creating such institutions in more than a dozen states ranging from Empire State College in New York to Metropolitan University in Minneapolis-St. Paul. In most cases of such major innovation either federal money or foundation money has already been committed prior to state support. Eventually the state, more often than not, picks up the full costs as the other funding sources lose interest or else recognize that they have achieved the objective of getting the program or institution underway.

In 1972 the federal government created the Fund for Innovation in Postsecondary Education. It has expended about $10 to $12 million a year on projects that institutions initiate. Funds are granted on a competitive basis with peer groups reviewing the proposals. Other federal agencies also use funds to support programs of a new or different character, for example, the National Science Foundation, the National Institute of Health, and the National Institute for Mental Health. Normally, however, the federal government supports its own program priorities only for a few years. Then it is expected that the institution will build into its budget the ongoing support required. Partly as a reaction to this temporary or incentive funding practice, some state governments have begun to reappropriate federal funds through their own legislatures in order to review the purposes of the federal programs and to withhold approval when spending seems incongruent with state objectives. Institutions see this practice as another chance for the state to place further controls on institutions, a very likely outcome since the state intent would require the federal funds to be rejected unless the program itself also met certain state needs.

Foundations have the justifiable reputation for providing the seed money which has brought much change and innovation in higher education. Again, as with the federal government, the funds are usually granted as incentives for short terms of two or three years. Often, though, the foundations take higher risks and support more radical innovations than the federal agencies. An outstanding example or two illustrates this point. The Ford Foundation provided over $75 million in about twelve years for experiments with television as a delivery system for education. Much of what is done through television today for higher education can be traced back to that original and, at the time, daring innovational experiment. The Carnegie Corporation created centers for research and funded major innovations in a large number of institutions for periods of five years or more. The Lilly Endowment recently expended large sums to encourage faculty evaluation and development in both private and public institutions.

A survey of the over 3,000 college and university presidents, comparing the changes which occurred in the five years before 1975 with those expected to occur from then to 1980, indicated that only a small fraction of institutions looked to much change between the two time periods. Most presidents projected mere extensions of what they had been doing between 1970 and 1975.

Changes estimated most frequently were in recruitment (of older students, evening students, and in continuing education) along with improved management practices for internal operation control.[9]

It is true that faculty senates are conservative, while presidents do not want to rock the boat during their relatively short tenures, and faculty unions create conditions inimical to major change in program or practice. Nevertheless, change and innovation continue without their active support. Overwhelming these conservative forces is the vast diversity of institutions and programs offered, the devotion of community colleges to provide everchanging services to their localities, and the pledge of the universities to engage in research and knowledge production through routine change which, over time, causes accretionary but drastic revisions in the roles of institutions and the programs which they offer. This incremental and largely unplanned approach has created the main revisions in courses, programs, and delivery methods.

If existing institutions do not respond to a new felt need in the society, one or more new institutions spring up to meet the challenge. Existing institutions now begin to recognize, as their enrollments level off or decline while the number of college age youth increases, that they must revise and initiate programs or be subject to decline and possible oblivion. With the advent of new technologies—such as video tapes and cassettes and computers which provide interaction instruction—even staid faculty and institutions realize that for many change is in the offing if not already occurring.

The United States is not as strongly committed to one institutional type—the university—as are most of the other countries of the western world. Rather, we support and nurture new types of institutions (the community college growth in the past thirty years being the most exemplary) and many forms of instruction. We tolerate and support the new even to the point of encouraging "faculty development." That in itself may become the greatest innovation of all. In order to meet the social goals of educating more minority persons and more women, most institutions have responded with new programs, new admissions policies, or additional student funding. As noted previously, these changes have largely succeeded by any criteria.

Extending Knowledge and Research

Of all the institutions of higher education, about two-hundred are recognized as having substantial graduate degrees and research capability. Fewer than fifty of the major universities obtain the majority of all funds allocated for research from all sources. The fifty comprise both public and private institutions most of which have a long and distinguished record of contributing to basic knowledge. The past success of these internationally renowned universities does not diminish the aspirations nor the actual research efforts of individual faculty members in hundreds of other institutions of virtually all types. A substantial amount of research is performed in the higher education setting even if the top fifty institutions are not considered.

Funding for research derives from a variety of sources with the largest share provided by the federal government, followed by state government, industry, and foundations. Each of these sources may provide the funds on a grant or contract basis for specified research. The major federal agencies set up proposal competitions for funds in designated research areas or on fairly specific problems. The meeting of deadline dates is followed by a review of each proposal by peer groups from the universities and other research agencies. A relatively small percentage of proposals submitted for any single competition receive funding (depending on the agency, from 5 to 20 percent).

Increasingly, federal contracts and grants carry with them conditions for the expenditure of funds—not so much on detailing research assumptions or objectives, but rather on such matters as fair labor standards, affirmative action, protection of minorities, and the protection of human subjects used in some types of research. The management of research projects is becoming much more complicated, resulting in more supervision and a great deal of reporting on administrative procedures.

This federal pattern of competition, peer review, and, even in a few cases, conditions or ties applies to industrial funding as well as funding from the major foundations. However, reporting is usually far less onerous and monitoring of research progress is less omnipresent than that for federal funding.

The states also fund particular research efforts and at times pass statutes or add amendments to appropriation bills for universities requiring that certain funds be spent on a very specific research effort—for example, controlling a virus attacking cotton plants, or improving a variety of wine grape. For the most part, however, state funds which can be identified as research monies find their way to the institutions through the budget for instruction. The major public research universities allow each regular full-time faculty member a certain amount of time off from teaching duties (50 percent or even more in most of these institutions) in order to conduct research. The funds for this "time off for research" constitute a substantial proportion of a university budget and have no strings or conditions attached since they go for regular faculty salaries. The state seldom funds more than a very small fraction of the actual research projects above this salary subsidy, except in agriculture.

Agencies other than the universities also compete for the same research funds that attract the attention of faculty members. The Rand Corporation, Battelle Institute, The Brookings Institution, and Bell Laboratories provide examples of nonprofit organizations formed for the sold purpose of conducting research, often policy-oriented. Still other agencies which perform services for higher education such as the College Entrance Examination Board, the Educational Testing Service, and the Education Commission of the States also maintain research components and compete for project funds.

All of these research organizations, staffed with highly trained university graduates, find themselves in competition for the same funds, thus potentially increasing the quality of research design and subsequent results. They also gear their proposals toward the research objectives that the funding agency more or less identifies. Some agencies such as the National Science Foundation and the National Institute of Health organize their research efforts under certain broad categories and then set objectives within each category. The field researchers may then compete through their own initiative by making concrete proposals. Foundations and industry also favor certain types or emphases of research over others. Part of the success in the competition lies in knowing these institutional priorities.

In addition, most of the federal agencies, but not usually the foundations, develop fairly specific high-priority proposals for research. The rough design and set of objectives is sent to the field in the form of an RFP (Request for Proposal). The research agencies then compete in design, methodology, and resources to obtain the research contract. Again peer review largely determines contract awards although some RFPs are written in such ways that only a very few or perhaps a single research agency would have the personnel, data banks, or other resources necessary to conduct the research.

Many researchers and a majority of those in the universities whose mission is to "extend knowledge," claim that too much of the research effort is directed toward specific short-term operational objectives and not enough toward basic research.[10] The funding agencies often find themselves under pressure from their governing bodies (Congress, legislature, governing board, board of directors) to produce results to solve concrete problems of social priority. Agency personnel (also university-trained) recognize the need for basic research on which more applied types of research can be grounded, so they often sympathize with university researchers. But they must also placate the funding authorities. This is an endless battle since basic and applied research have such great overlapping components and neither has been very clearly defined. Yet those within the university assume that more and more available research funds go to outside research agencies primarily because of their applied rather than basic research character.

Pressure from within universities for extending knowledge through research has increased steadily since the turn of the last century. Faculty members in the large research universities receive promotions, merit increases, and tenure largely on the basis of their productivity in research and scholarly writing. While, in the past few years, teaching has become a somewhat more important component in such personnel matters, research and writing continue to be the major criteria for faculty committees assessing their colleagues' merits. Hence the competition for research funds touches not only faculty colleagues in other universities and institutes, but also the faculty member in the next office.

University contributions to the advancement of knowledge go beyond the research act itself. Faculty preoccupation with research carries with it the training of graduate advisees and assistants in research design, methodology, and management. Statistics and computer programming capabilities are considered desirable by-product attributes of the well-trained doctoral graduate in all but a few disciplinary areas. Perhaps the most beneficial results of university emphasis on research are the graduates who find their way into a variety of basic and applied research positions in government, industry, and business.

The results of university research need not be related here, for the technology and knowledge necessary to maintain this nation as a democratic society and as one of the most powerful nations of the world — economically, militarily, and culturally — speaks of that success. Every major university could list many significant contributions as a result of its research, whether it be genetic engineering or developing a square tomato. Contributions to world knowledge can be exemplified by the number of Nobel and other international prizes awarded to university scholars in this country, far exceeding the number for any other country in the sciences and medicine. A single leading university may have a half dozen Nobel prize winners.

The knowledge generated by research appears in the ever expanding number of scientific journals, papers given at myriad conferences, and in books which may be translated into several languages. Keeping up with these new developments poses a growing and serious problem for scholars. One professor of materials research at a midwestern university has indicated that by the time one of his graduate students obtains his degree, the knowledge gained in his specialization during his undergraduate years is already obsolete.

Cultural Contributions

Culture defined in a broad sense encompasses most of what is discussed in this paper. However, in this section we will define it as the fine and performing arts. Almost all college or university level institutions in the nation offer a variety of opportunities for the study of music, art, drama, poetry, and literature. Most institutions provide concerts, plays, recitals, readings, and exhibits. A few institutions specialize in a single cultural subject, a school of art or a school of music not connected with a university or a college which also offers the general liberal arts subjects. Whatever the type of institution, the enrollments in these cultural areas fluctuate as the tastes of Americans change and increase as more leisure and affluence allow for more enjoyment of these life-fulfilling activities. One can say that in any community where a college makes its arts known and open to the public, the quality of life in that community greatly improves.

The financial support for these activities again comes from a variety of sources, with private philanthropy playing a larger role here than in other functions or services of higher education institutions. State funds provide the basic buildings and teaching resources in the public institutions, although performing arts centers may be built from private gifts. Often both public and private funds are comingled to achieve this objective. In the last fifteen years more colleges and universities have added cultural facilities to their campuses than in all previous history of the institutions. To further advance the performing arts, the federal government has established the National Endowment for the Humanities and the Federal Council on the Arts and Humanities, thus providing sources of continuing funding for both public and private colleges and universities as well as other organizations specializing in the performing arts.

One cannot say that the universities and colleges turn out all the finest artists, the best musicians, or the most capable dramatists, as would be said of scientists and engineers, for example. Many of the best artists receive private tutoring (often from university or college professors, but more often from a master who has turned to private teaching) either to supplement collegiate training or to supplant it altogether. The students who wish to savor the rewards of a fine arts performance or exhibit find many courses in the arts, most of which fall within the work acceptable for a bachelor's degree.

Other Contributions

Sports. Beyond the enrichment which the fine arts provide, one finds the higher institutions contributing substantially to the training and development of amateur and professional athletes. Ordinary courses in physical education offer the student opportunity to learn tennis, baseball, field hockey, soccer, track skills, swimming, gymnastics, and even dancing. Intercollegiate team sports such as football, baseball, track, soccer, and basketball draw millions of spectators to college and university campuses throughout the academic year.

Virtually all the professional sports teams now have a majority or are fully staffed by athletes who got their final training at an institution of higher education. Whereas in other countries athletic unions and clubs often provide the most opportunity for building athletic proficiency, in the United States this expert training largely comes from the various types of two-year and four-year colleges and universities. A few such institutions do not engage in intercollegiate competitions because of the expense, but they often emphasize intramural sports activities more fully than other schools.

Citizenship Improvement. General population surveys consistently show that persons who have attended college or received a degree participate actively and provide leadership in a great variety of civic and volunteer service enterprises. Social service clubs and associations which raise funds for many health, welfare, and recreational functions are led by the college educated. We find that the more education an individual has the more volunteer work he or she will engage in.[11] Political organizations too receive their leadership and active membership from degree-holding citizens. Moreover, the college educated vote in larger numbers and in greater proportions than do the noncollege educated.[12]

While motivation and ability cannot be fully attributed to a college education (for the nation developed to this point with much lower average levels of education), the complexities of modern societies almost demand a more thorough grounding in sociology, political science, and economics than could generally be acquired outside the traditional learning centers. Howard Bowen summarizes the college effects on citizenship as follows:[13]

> It produces moderate shifts toward liberal views and ideological thinking, toward greater interest, information, and involvement in political and public affairs, and toward greater inclination to vote. Also, college-educated people are more active than others in community affairs. Regarding crime, educated people are less prone than others to ordinary criminal activity, but the effect of higher education on "white-collar crime" or other antisocial behavior is unclear.

Other Outcomes. Bowen draws comprehensively on the research and literature relating to almost all aspects of educational outcomes and gives an optimistic, favorable rating to colleges and universities.[14] His book, *Investment in Learning*, covers the full range of traditional liberal arts objectives—developing the whole man in his tolerance, creativity, wisdom, and emotional and moral attributes—in each case concluding from the evidence that higher education and its contributions to the individual and society in other than economic returns far outweigh the sheer economic benefits. He would conclude that while some results attributed to higher education may derive from other social experiences and forces, college education certainly improves societal and personal well-being.

Excellence and Quality

Philosophers and scholars from Plato to Thomas Jefferson, Bernard Shaw and Bertrand Russell to John Gardner have assessed the problems of achieving excellence in a society committed to a democratic mode. Each vote is equal in a narrow political sense, regardless of the voter's educational qualifications, ability, or intelligence. Citizens must have equal rights, including the opportunity for higher learning. But this presents the democratic society with the great problems inherent in differing abilities while trying to encourage excellence and high quality in those who are more capable.

The great expansion in enrollments allowing mass higher education brought with it a concomitant desire by all who entered to obtain a degree or certificate. Pressures in the elementary and secondary schools resulted in young people being moved up grade by grade without having achieved any particular level of reading, writing, mathematics, or other capability. The result has been a decided increase in the proportion of secondary school graduates who, by traditional standards, function at lower levels of literacy and mathematical capability than that expected of high school graduates. This slippage is serious enough by itself but when coupled with open admission policies of certain higher education institutions, it produces entering students who are less prepared than in the past. The functions of some higher institutions attempting to cope with these students were changed to accommodate their needs. Remedial education, new, specially designed programs requiring less rigor to complete, and the practice of lowering the grading standards each contributed to graduates of two- and four-year colleges who fell short of the traditional standards.

Concurrently, with a plentiful supply of possible applicants, other colleges and universities took the opportunity to sharpen and improve the quality of their programs and the requirements for graduation. Hence, in traditional terms, the range in quality of institutions today is as great as at any time in the nation's history. Some critics deplore the loss of traditional outcomes for all students while others claim that such diversity in institutional function and practice results in a greater benefit to society. What can be the measure of excellence in a pluralistic, democratic society that requires persons with sufficient talents and skills to search for the origins of the earth, to manage large and small enterprises, or to repair a TV set? John Gardner answered a part of this question when he stated:[15]

> ... we need a broad conception of standards embracing many kinds of excellence at many levels. This is the only conception of excellence that fully accords with the richly varied potentialities of mankind, and it is the only one that will permit large numbers of Americans to strive for and achieve excellence in forms accessible to them....

He goes on to state that the individual "... must seek the kind of education that will open *his* eyes, stimulate *his* mind and unlock *his* potentialities." Does American higher education achieve these outcomes?

The evidence previously presented shows a large measure of success that could hardly have been achieved without a certain level of excellence in the colleges and universities. This does not mean, however, that all institutions, all programs, or all faculty are excellent. The diversity which the institutions represent provides an array of opportunities for specializing in almost every human endeavor. Some of these are excellent; some not.

The measures used for determining quality have generally been process-related rather than outcome-related. We examine, for example, the credentials, training, and experience of faculty members, the number of volumes in the library, the student-faculty ratio, and the dollar expenditure per student as proxies for outcomes. Of course, many outcomes are not measurable. An alternative method seeks the judgment of peers in the field. Roose and Cartter for the American Council on Education sought the opinion of deans and scholars across the nation in rating most of the doctoral programs in the liberal arts and sciences.[16] Such surveys are criticized because of the bias of the individuals surveyed, because an institution may not offer programs on which the rating is based (the reason the University of California at Berkeley rated over Harvard), and because the sheer number of graduates of a program (who now vote from the field) may weight opinion towards that program rather than one which awards fewer degrees of higher quality.

Despite the deficiencies in the measure used for determining a quality institution or a quality level of teaching, both faculty members and students generally can relate the names of a dozen or so institutions which they consider to be excellent. With rare exceptions, the conventional wisdom supports both the proxies mentioned earlier and the opinion survey method of assessing quality in an institution.

However, agreement on which are the best institutions does not indicate the level of quality of higher education across the land. In the past three years in particular, a spate of assessments by scholars has resulted in a tightening of standards in many if not most colleges and universities. More courses are required rather than left to the option of students; courses themselves require more demanding work of the student. Pass/fail options give way to traditional grading standards, and professors become less lenient in grading student work. This activity, which remains in nascent but growing stages in most institutions, reflects real concern by the higher education community that standards of quality deteriorated during the process of shifting from elite to mass education. The question which remains as this reassessment continues is the effect that the declining number of students in the traditional college age-group (eighteen to twenty-two years old) will have on maintaining tougher standards. The evidence from the early 1970s, when enrollment fell briskly for some institutions, would indicate that at least some institutions will do "almost anything" to maintain their enrollment, and thus, their funding base. The better institutions will have less difficulty in obtaining students who fit or almost fit their standards for entrance, while the poorer ones, by lowering standards to attract student numbers, may well become poorer yet in both quality and funds. Students tend to go to the older, more pretigious schools, whatever locality they live in, with the result that the newer institutions which were created to fill the needs of the 1960s become the most vulnerable to enrollment declines — almost regardless of faculty quality, library size, or expenditure per student (which under the circumstances tends to increase each year as enrollment drops). The United States has met the challenge of increased enrollment and now seeks to improve quality in both traditional and new modes of delivery.

System Efficiency and Management

Of all the demands placed on higher educational systems none are more pervasive nor onerous than those requiring more efficiency, accountability, and productivity. Colleges and universities have more or less accomodated the strident urgings of outside groups for greater access, special programs for minorities, affirmative action, and innovations to meet new needs. But university and college leaders are puzzled and frustrated by charges of inefficiency and lack of management expertise. In the first place, the different levels of government and their many agencies, as well as public and private organizations — each urges the colleges and universities with whom it deals to be accountable or efficient in particular ways, sometimes incompatible, sometimes inconsistent. Each group thinks its own priorities are paramount; but the university or college tries to respond to each demand in some practical, satisfactory way. Secondly, the students and their parents, who by no means agree about what the college or university should be doing, nevertheless assert their separate, divergent requests for change and action in order to force more accountability. Their goals are often quite different from those of public officials who worry more about student-faculty ratios, faculty productivity in student credit hours, research versus undergraduate teaching, and unnecessary overlapping and duplication in programs; the students and parents worry about access, getting the right program, staying in college with its frightening costs, and obtaining a job after graduating. The range of groups interested in higher education, its processes, and its outcomes is only exceeded by the number of ways the many constituencies of higher education expect the institutions to be accountable and efficient.

Both the federal government and the states step up regulations for increasing efficiency in management and practice in a variety of ways, each of which requires institutions to take particular substantive actions or to change procedures. The institutions then must prepare elaborate reports on their accomplishments for the government agency. Both public and private institutions are affected, although the degree to which states intervene in private college affairs falls far short of that for the public institutions.

In this section, we will discuss some elements of efficiency, management, and accountability to determine the degree to which higher institutions have or have not been responsive to their several constituencies. The discussion focuses on three aspects of the problem—planning, administration, and coordination. Both structural organizational elements and substantive programmatic elements are characteristic of each area. We will discuss the elements of efficiency at the federal level first and then turn to the states.

Federal Government

As David Henry has stated, the federal government has little legal jurisdiction over colleges and universities; rather it asserts its priorities and conditions through money grants and contracts which it offers to students and to institutions and their faculties. Some grant conditions require planning by the organization or the state government; others put demands on administrative and procedural activities, and a few require coordination with other federal or state agencies.

Planning

Henry properly describes the lack of comprehensive federal planning for higher education. Undeniably, major statutes which set up programs to be funded for five years or longer inherently require a high degree of planning. The aggregation of such separate statutes, however important, does not add up to a national plan. Indeed, critical scholars delight in pointing out the incongruities and inconsistencies highlighted by the divergent character of major federal programs. Each federal agency proposes statutes to support programs on its own priorities, with relatively little reference to other agency plans. Congressional substantive committees have not been foresighted or powerful enough to bring the diverse programs into a coherent whole. This deficiency arises from the fact that proposals come before Congress at different times and partly from the rapidly changing circumstances — economic and social — which confront Congress in considering an important bill this year as compared with those passed in previous years. While the Executive Office of the President through the Office of Management and Budget is technically the coordinator of all federal programs, it falls short of predicting what the Congress will do on specific programs, especially those of high political salience and high cost. The result has been very little federal planning and a lack of coherency among the many programs, literally hundreds, put into effect. Federal planning is inefficient, however effective individual programs may be in carrying out particular objectives.

David Henry mentions the national associations — of institutions, of faculties, of administrators — as helping to fill the void in federal planning. He correctly asserts that they do so in part; however, each of these organizations, just as separate federal agencies, has its own set of assumptions, desired directions, and long-run objectives. Collectively, such commission and organization studies do no more to create a comprehensive national plan than does the federal government itself. Individually, these commission reports may be exemplary in dealing with a subject area, one of these being the 1974 report of the National Board on Graduate Education, recognized as exceptionally farsighted and realistic but atypical in its failure to be self-serving and parochial in outlook as are many such reports.

The last government-commission report on higher education was that of the Commission on Financing Postsecondary Education; faced with volatile conflicting forces, the commission, in its wisdom, decided not to make any recommendations but rather to discuss the issues. Very little change resulted from the report and certainly no new programs for federal financing of postsecondary education. It had been almost twenty years since the last report, so federal commissions have not really been effective planners since the beginning of the enrollment expansion period. No change in this condition is indicated on the immediate horizon.

Administration

Perhaps the requirements which are most apparent to institutions and their leaders are the many, divergent, and complex standards imposed by federal agencies administering programs. The traditional conditions of meeting certain financial, accounting, and personnel requirements, while onerous, were considered legitimate requests by a government that was furnishing public funds. When these conditions were recently augmented by dozens of others — relating to such things as equal opportunity, affirmative action, fair labor standards, and protection of human subjects in research — data gathering and reporting workloads reached somewhat staggering proportions for institutions involved with many federal programs. The large universities, which were hardest hit by these conditions, share their anguish with all other institutions which must report on some practices covered by general law, such as affirmative action.

The interventions into both procedural matters and substantive affairs have become sufficiently loathsome to warrant the creation of a commission to investigate the relationships of government and higher education; the commission has been funded by the Sloan Foundation. The study is to last three years at a cost of several million dollars. The focus primarily falls on the federal government although, as discussed later, the states continue to increase their intervention in bolder ways than does the federal government.

Through such conditional devices, the federal government attempts to improve efficiency (as the federal administering agency sees it) and to bring some uniformity to program administration across the nation. Conditional grants-in-aid are old devices but they have increased in sheer numbers for higher education to the point where federal financial incentives tend to determine a recognizable fraction of state higher educational policy. The objectives of the federal legislation usually are acceptable to the higher education community but may be closely questioned by governors and legislators who see state power yielding to federal pressure. The alternative method — the federal government administering the programs out of a federal office in each state or region — would be a greater anathema to state officials and to those in higher education institutions. Thus, despite the criticism, the desire for funds by the colleges and universities leads them to request and accept funding, even when it entails burdensome reporting procedures.

Coordination

The lack of comprehensive planning, with myriad agencies being involved in many special programs with multiple objectives, also prevents efficient administration of the whole federal effort. It is piecemeal administration at best, at times bordering on the chaotic. Have these practices resulted in more efficiency, more productivity, and better management for higher education?

Modern system management concerned with efficiency and productivity would have all the planning and administrative activities coordinated by a single overarching agency. None exists at the federal level for higher education although some attempts have been made to improve interagency coordination of programs and even administration. As David Henry states, interagency councils have been established to try to achieve coordination where none previously existed. Yet the federal councils have no direct authority to control the agencies represented, rather only power to enlighten, cajole, and suggest model ways of accomplishing coordinative objectives. Each agency then decides for itself the degree to which it will comply. Since the programs each agency administers represent a special priority of that agency, the difficulties in obtaining council agreement on courses of action become very difficult and compliance is almost an impossibility. Each agency, with its political constituencies and with certain power in government circles, protects its own territory, caring little for overall coordination or efficiency (even if that were to be the real outcome) or the effects of its program on those administered by other agencies. Planning and coordination are interrelated, and the reasons for the failure of one also account for the failure of the other.

Conflicting policies embedded in hundreds of different programs do not necessarily result in inefficient, nonproductive, or inimical outcomes for higher education. Indeed, the oppositie conclusion can be reasonably argued. Experience indicates that diversity of funding sources increases the autonomy of the institutions. Diversity of program funding sources also allows a greater degree of freedom for each college or university or each state, as the case may be, to develop the program to fit local conditions and circumstances, epitomized by distinctive features which might readily be lost with greater coordination and uniform administration.

For university research, the chief funding source is the federal government through its uncoordinated agencies and programs. The diversity of present research projects belies the idea that by serious, comprehensive coordination a more effective research effort might be undertaken. This is particularly true for the basic research area to which universities commit themselves, rather than for operational research which may require a high degree of coordination. Program and institutional diversity, possibly the greatest strength of American higher education, seems encouraged by the lack of a single national policy or a specific set of national objectives.

Proposals for a federal department of education, separate from the Department of Health, Education, and Welfare (HEW), have received little political support. Ostensibly, such a department would attempt much greater coordination—having under its aegis some programs now found in a number of other federal departments as well as those scattered about in HEW. Administrative coordination might be improved in that manner but long-range planning would have little better odds for improvement than under present auspices. The education-related programs of the present twenty-nine agencies would not be put in the new department; they could not, politically, be wrested away from the existing bases. So disparate objectives and practices would continue, albeit perhaps without the same vigor as at present. Also the programs now officially under the Office of Education have not themselves ever been coordinated either in planning or operations. And the regional offices of HEW have made that condition even worse by following their own priorities and proclivities in administering some programs.

One may conclude that federal funding of colleges and universities is relatively poorly planned as a system and also rather poorly and expensively administered but that many, if not a majority, of the programs, have surprisingly effective results. Part of that success may result from the federal delegation of planning and administration to the states which have, under the Constitution, the responsibility for education, including higher education.

State Governments

State legal responsibility, as noted in John Shea's statement, historically carried with it the continuing lion's share of funding for the public colleges and universities, with federal funding fluctuating according to the caprices of federal manpower or service needs. The states and their agencies for planning, administration, and coordination have thus built up a far more intimate relationship with institutions than has the federal government. For public institutions the state deals with literally thousands of matters each year. In each case, the state is able to affect how the matter is given priority, funds, and implementing support.

Planning

States have conducted surveys of need of comprehensive planning for forty or more years. Early plans dealt primarily with structure and very little, if any, with funding programs. As the enrollment bulge of the 1950s and 60s came upon the states, the nature of plans and the process shifted considerably toward more comprehensive planning and more participation by several constituencies served by colleges and universities. By the late 1960s almost every state had a "master plan," which had been developed within the previous five years. However, as enrollments began to decline unexpectedly and disillusionment set in for higher education planners, agencies backed away from large-scale plans in favor of special studies for incremental changes in program areas, such as medicine or doctoral studies, without pretense that collectively these individual studies added up to a total plan. About 1975, as the future picture of enrollment became clearer (the downturn after 1980 being accepted as a very probable reality) and the attitude of policy makers became rather steady, more comprehensive plans once again became the order of the day. The Education Commission of the States, the Center for Research and Development at Berkeley, and the Carnegie Commission helped to focus attention on the need for better long-range planning and improved procedures for accomplishing it. Patrick, Callan, in looking to enrollment and funding patterns and the age groups likely to attend colleges and universities in the 1980s, cited the benefits of planning in this new and very different era for higher education. He stated:[17]

> Boards that commit considerable energy and resources to planning are more likely to have a clear sense of priorities from which strategies for guiding state systems through a difficult era can be achieved. Boards that develop effective planning processes are more likely to be cognizant of the concerns and aspirations of their internal and external constituencies. And boards that place heavy emphasis on planning are likely to be better aware of their needs in filling key staff posi-

tions.... Planning can lend itself to the raising of fundamental questions of purposes, policies and priorities in a way that other managerial functions cannot....

The result has been new attention to planning by the states, normally through the state coordinating or statewide governing board for higher education but also by legislatures, outside consulting firms, and governor's commissions. These new planning efforts confront the reality that the college-age group is expected to decline in numbers by 23 percent between 1980 and 1993 with consequent reductions in the number of institutions or the number of programs required. New York, Washington, and Florida among other states have asked for reductions in the number of doctoral programs in specific disciplinary areas. Other plans have led to recommendations for closure or partial consolidation of institutions in Montana and South Dakota. After the 1968-75 period of little planning, the state agencies have made serious attempts to face the future in much more realistic ways. These new plans have widespread constituency involvement, being conducted through a series of task forces with institutional faculty, administrative, and student membership, as well as citizens and general advisory committees to help in the final formulation of a plan for approval by the board of higher education or its equivalent. Most plans require some, but not much, legislation—unless the organizational structure or governance of the system is to be changed. The agencies themselves often enforce provisions of the plan in cooperation with the institutions, and with the very real but often unstated backing of the governor and legislature.

Increasingly, the planning process includes the private institutions along with the public. The federal grants for 1202 Commissions for planning aided this endeavor, but many states had already begun to include private colleges in their planning. Now private and proprietary schools have representation on the committees and boards and are included in the substantive issues of the plan itself. This inclusion and cooperation of private institutions is accelerating as state funds are allocated to private higher education either in the form of student grants or capitation grants to the institutions. The theory is that as private institutions receive state funds to that extent they become public and can be subjected to the same planning and development constraints as the public institutions.

Coordination

Since planning and coordination at the state level are, with few exceptions, carried on by the same agency, the two functions are often grouped together for analyses. Coordination, however, includes a great deal more than planning, and the agencies which have coordinative powers also have means for enforcing the provisions of master plans. The state agencies used for coordinating purposes were classified by this author first in 1959,[18] and later by many others who added refinements without much changing the basic character of the classes. The classes of agencies mentioned by Henry follow the old pattern. Of these agency types, experience and research show rather unequivocally that the state coordinating board with regulatory powers has the best record of planning and has as good a record of coordinating budgets and programs as the statewide governing boards. Neither voluntary organizations nor those with advisory powers have generally had equivalent influence, although both states of Washington and Maryland are clearly exceptions.

Coordination is generally thought to include not only the planning function as a continuous cyclical process, but also and perhaps more importantly for specific influence on current policy, a budget review function and a program review function of new and existing programs. Miscellaneous other matters such as minimum admission standards, enrollment ceilings for institutions, and construction standards may be numbered among the array of activities which are characteristic of the coordinating agencies.

The question of whether coordinating agencies infringe on the autonomy of the institutions has an easy answer—yes. That is their very reason for being. They are to reduce areas of overlaps and duplication in programs, to promote innovations, to review budgets for their conformance to master plan objectives, and to bring general order to the state system of higher education. In these endeavors, to one degree or another, the traditional autonomy of the institution to go its own way regardless of the consequences to other institutions or to students outside its doors generally has given way to much more control, review, and outright veto of college or university objectives.

The state master plan relates the role and mission of each public college and university, and often indicates the general role of private institutions. As long as budget items, new program proposals, and new expenditure requests for equipment fall within the boundaries of the role and mission statement in the plan, the institution finds relatively little reason to confront the central state coordinating office. However, each departure from the plan or a move to encompass some area of programming or campus development not in the plan calls for a thorough review and much discussion, with the possibility that the item may be given a negative recommendation or even transferred to another institution whose role is seen as more appropriate for the function. Institutions have a rather parochial perspective about what their role is in the state system while the state agency comprehends all institutional missions, planned statewide objectives, and the funding available for higher education. Hence, conflict and long disagreements often do occur between the central agency and an institution. But whom does the autonomy of an institution benefit: the students? the faculty? the administrative staffs? the state? the society? The coordinating agency, standing between the institutions and the legislative and executive branches of government is established to answer this question. Not surprisingly, the answer sometimes goes against the desires of particular institutions, presumably in favor of a broader state interest.

For coordination, as for planning, the agencies tend to set up interinstitutional committees and task forces with a diversified membership of students, faculty, administrators, and citizens.

Coordination will be discussed further in the section following on administration, but here we will consider two other elements of coordinative effort. First, the state group of colleges and universities, as Professor Henry observed, is often divided into subsystems, usually but not always, of similar types of institutions. Each subsystem may have its own governing board, coordinative procedures, and conduct planning and operational activities with the authority to govern in addition to the authority to coordinate. These very powerful boards have almost absolute control over the development of each campus and each program. They pass upon the budgets, new programs, and buildings proposed with clear powers to say either yes or no. Their recommendations on matters of statewide interest go to the state coordinating board and there the "system of systems" is made operative.

Research on the effectiveness of state boards and subsystem

boards is somewhat ambiguous. An accurate description of what the boards do in practice does not lead to agreement on their effectiveness. Reviewers of such research findings may come up with almost opposite conclusions. Those writers, most of whom have not done field research or who side with the large research university of a state, tend to favor a single statewide governing board for all institutions—the epitome of centralization, with ultimate, systematic control over every campus within the system. The political science researchers give the nod of "most effective" to the state coordinating agency with regulatory powers, partly because they observe the single governing board representing only the most powerful institutions, partly because the record shows that the state college type of institution and the community colleges fare better in states with coordinating boards, and partly because coordinating agencies hold better records for statewide planning including private higher education as well as public. Nevertheless, state legislatures in the recent period of financial depression reassessed the potential control and efficiency which a single board could bring to the public system. Many bills were introduced in legislatures to change the fundamental structures, but none have passed in the past five years. Legislatures and governors hesitate because they recognize that a single governing board for public institutions cannot be the agent for planning for the private and proprietary institutions, for dispensing funds to private institutions or to all students in the state, or for acting as the spokesman for higher education. The issue is ongoing and will be resolved not by research but the political forces at work in each state—whatever the merits of either method of achieving coordination.

The policy issues before all these agencies in the states have been summarized and listed by subject area and in priority order by the State Higher Education Executive Officers (SHEEO), the directors of the state agencies. In 1977, the first ten items on the list of issues were: student aid, appropriations, enrollments, comprehensive and master planning (all of which were the first four the previous year as well), community colleges, tuition and fees, 1202 commissions, continuing adult education, and program review. In assessing which type agency ought to be the chief coordinating agency for a state, an evaluation of these issues and the relative likelihood of their being resolved by each type could give some clue for coordinative direction. Of the issues listed, only half could be dealt with on a full statewide basis by a single governing board for all the public institutions, while every one of them could be handled by an advisory or regulatory coordinating board.

Administration

The agencies for coordination and planning also have considerable impact on several of the administrative areas considered in this paper. When one considers administration of systems as diversified and loosely organized as those in the United States, attention must drift from institution to system board, to coordinating board, and on to the legislature and the governor, especially their professional staff. The interrelationships among these several agencies become apparent in considering each administrative area.

Budgeting and Allocation of Funds. For private institutions a budget is the proposed expenditure program for the following year. The income to be derived for fulfilling budget expectations comes primarily from tuition in most institutions, from gifts and grants, from government (federal and state), and some from endowment income in a few of the wealthier colleges and universities. The problem for the private institution is to raise sufficient funds to maintain the operation from year to year. The budget may be rather static except for inflation factors and adjustments in salaries. Funds are raised to meet these changes as well to continue last year's budget. The leadership of the institution generally assumes responsibility for this task. The president and his development officer raise the funds and with the business officer determine the parameters of the budget for approval by the institutional governing board. The procedure for formulating and obtaining approval of the budget seems simple in relation to state processes, but obtaining funds sufficient to operate the institution for another year provides a common base of concern for both the public and private college administrators.

The leaders of public colleges form their budgets very much as their private counterparts; assume continuation of last year's requests, receive new proposals from the academic departments and research centers, review proposals with some faculty committee, set priorities among the new items, adjust all items for inflation, make up the line item or program budget, and submit it to request funds from the government.

The form and content of the budget is governed by procedures handed down by the budget office of the governor or by the state coordinating board, or both. The budget is reviewed by the local governing board of the institution or system and passed up to the state level. Usually the request receives first review and comment by the coordinating board, often after lengthy hearings and negotiations with the leaders of each institution. The coordinating board provides a thorough substantive review of all new items or programs, cuts some requests, and consolidates results into a combined budget for all the public institutions. Normally in this process each institution maintains its identity in the documentary material and also later on as the request goes to the governor's budget office and the staff agencies of the legislature. In states with a single governing board, the individual campuses may or may not be separately identified with particular budget amounts after board review. If not, the political arms pass on the consolidated budget and after appropriation, the board allocates the funds to the individual institutions, usually in proportion to the amount initially recommended by the board.

The state executive budget office, also staffed with professionally trained analysts, reviews the budgets primarily for total amounts of money and dwells on individual items or programs only occasionally. This practice varies by state, however, and in a few every item is reviewed at least as carefully by this staff as by the coordinating board. The higher education budget is then made a part of the governor's executive budget which goes forward to the legislature for its action. Several different legislative staff agencies may review the budget for higher education, sometimes as many as three. Legislative reviews concentrate on programmatic aspects with a few items of high political interest isolated for in-depth analysis. Again, as at the coordinating board and executive budget offices, the staff makes recommendations for adjustments in the amounts to be appropriated. Hearings are held by all of these offices and by the legislative appropriations committees in each house to obtain further information from institutional officers and the coordinators. Final decisions are then made in a conference committee representing the two houses of the legislature, voted on by the two houses, and then sent to the governor for signature. The governor may veto some items, or in some states he may have power to reduce the amount of money in items and frequently does so to bring the amounts back to those shown in the executive budget request. The money is then allocated to the institutions or to the systems governing board, usually in quarterly allotments. In most states, the institutions may spend the money without being bound by the specific items or amounts in the original request. That practice seems to be waning, however, and increasingly the legislative committees (sometimes the executive budget office) post-audit budget reviews to determine if institutions have spent the funds in accordance with listings in the initial request, usually made eighteen months or more before.

In 1977, after much research on state budgetary processes, the associates at the Berkeley Center concluded that the strength and control of legislative staffs were increasing very rapidly, outdistancing the influence and control over the budget which the coordinating boards were exercising, although the latter boards were also obtaining new power. The legislative power struggle with the governor over the budget and most substantive matters is a fairly recent phenomenon. Legislative committees have increased in power and in the number of their staff members as a weapon to fight that battle. In this power competition the colleges and universities, caught between these contending political forces, are reviewed not just by a coordinating agency, but again by the governor's office, two or three times by legislative staffs, and by the two appropriations committees. Moreover, the legislatures and some executive offices increasingly establish program audit committees to review programs of higher education as well as of other state services. These in-depth studies may take a year or two to complete, deal with a single major subject, and often result in recommendations for fundamental changes in institutional control or operation of the program, further resulting in funding changes. The number and technical character of the state level reviews threatens to increase even more in the immediate future. The Berkeley Center recommended that a clearer set of functions in budget review be adopted by the respective agencies and that as much redundancy as possible be eliminated.

Admission of Students. Institutions, both public and private, primarily maintain control over both the numbers and quality of students. In a few states, minimum levels of ability may be specified by law or regulation for each type of public institution with each campus making the decision on which students to admit. Statewide tests are not administered in any state for admissions purposes. A few state systems or subsystems also allow a student to apply to several institutions with a single application, expressing priority preferences of the campuses he wishes to attend. If the first choice cannot be met, the student has the option of admission to his second or third choice, if possible. These relatively new centralized admissions offices usually operate with computer assistance. They are increasing in number and appear to be a decided improvement in practice for the student. Of course, we should add that a student is free to apply to as many individual institutions as he or she wishes.

Admissions procedures have also been revised in order to admit minority persons who could not qualify under previous standards. The academic record of these entrants in some colleges equals that of regularly admitted students. This is another reason for the proportional growth of black students in college.

Selection of Faculty. The state does not set the standards nor does it participate in the process of selecting faculty for any institution. This institutional prerogative has seldom been violated by the state in any way. Within institutions the department faculty nominate the new faculty member. This recommendation is seldom overruled by a committee, the president, or the governing board. Departmental faculties tend to seek colleagues very much like themselves, that is, without widely varying philosophies or divergent views, although they attempt to identify the best qualified applicant. The greatest restraint in the period of financial stringency is the limitation of the level of professorship to which the recruit may be hired. The research universities have faculties composed 70 to 80 percent of doctorate holders. State colleges have fewer doctorate-holding faculty on average and community colleges, often by preference, do not recruit doctorates. They prefer faculty members trained to teach rather than to conduct scholarly research.

Development and Change in the Curriculum. Like the budget, the approval of new degree or certificate programs requires an increasingly elaborate and often contentious review process in public institutions. Yet the programmatic results still allow 85 percent of the students to say they are satisfied with their educational experience. Institutions, not central offices, generally control the arrangement and number of courses for a degree program. Programs proposed by faculty almost always require approval by the governing board and by the state coordinating board. The latter board provides only cursory review of undergraduate and less costly programs but reviews very carefully those at the graduate level, especially doctoral programs. Some states employ outside consultants to review each doctoral proposal, partly to get expert, objective advice and partly to avoid charges of favoritism if institutional requests vary in outcome. The governor's budget office may examine a new program if it is high cost, or if a good bit of publicity preceeded in the review process. Legislative committees are much more likely to review programs in detail even after they have been approved by other agencies. Occasionally, an institution will take to the legislature a proposal for a program which has been rejected by the coordinating board. In only a few instances does this political ploy work to the advantage of the institution.

Government increasingly has given lump sums of money, usually not large amounts, to coordinating or statewide boards in order to encourage innovation and change within the institutions. The latter compete for these funds by proposals, with awards made primarily on the basis of merit as seen by the coordinating staff or a panel of outside reviewers. Rarely, but occasionally, a legislature appropriates a specific sum to be used to start a school or a program favored by a single but powerful legislator. Over the years, almost every state has had a few examples of this kind.

Institutions would rather not have their proposals for new programs, and certainly not their existing programs, reviewed by any outside agency. However, the scheme described earlier has been applauded by students of higher education as well as the policy makers. The process avoids duplication of expensive, unnecessary programs and a more efficient system results from applying resources saved to more suitable programs. Legislative intervention during the appropriations process, and afterward in the post-audit, concern both the institutional leaders and those of the coordinating board. Legislative staffs, usually not well qualified for program review purposes, sometimes seem to make recommendations reflecting caprice rather than studied review. The turnover rates and pay scales of legislative staff mitigate against improvements in this situation during the immediate future.

Establishment of New Institutions. In nearly every state new private institutions are relatively easy to establish. Often only three to six people may take out incorporation papers, pay a small fee, and start a new college. No standards relating to curriculum, faculty, library, or other aspects of colleges or universities are applied prior to authorizing the college. Hence, even in the past ten years when some private institutions have failed, a greater number were created. Most are small and experimental but the state does not control those aspects either. Only when the college seeks accreditation will one of the regional, voluntary accrediting associations review the institution in considerable depth and determine whether or not to award accreditation. Accreditation becomes a valuable asset since federal and state fund usually do not go to unaccredited private colleges nor may students receive federal grants to attend them.

The creation of a public institution requires a very laborious staff and political process. During the 1950s and 1960s hundreds of new four-year and two-year colleges were created. At one time in the mid-sixties, one community college came into existence each week. But even then the process was not simple.

Today a new institution is likely to be proposed by the coordinating board or the statewide governing board, quite possibly in a master plan. A few community colleges are still formed under state law but with local city or district initiative. In almost every instance both the governor and legislature must approve a new institution. The process of application and hearing resembles that of budget review but other institutions as well as the politicians have an expressed interest in whether or not the new institution is created. The issue of new colleges becomes less important each year as enrollments level off, although as population centers arise in formerly rural areas pressures for a new educational institution may increase. Branch campuses of existing institutions appear likely to suffer the same fate: they will become a less important issue as enrollments level off. They too now require a series of approvals which seem unlikely to be obtained except in extraordinary circumstances.

Conclusion

The effectiveness of higher education in the United States results more from the wealth of the country, the commitment of individual faculty members, and the aspirations of administrators than from its efficiency. The system is highly productive in terms of graduates, research, and the public services it renders. Efficiency, however one may define it other than in terms of productivity, would not be a word ordinarily applied to describe the college and university system. Critics continue to call the system inefficient. Supporters and "in house" scholars and administrators can see the need for possible improvements but do not see that there is inefficiency.

Financial constraints in the early seventies brought many changes in practice both in management of resources and in program review and approval. Those developments led to much more efficiency as defined by central staffs and politicians and, given the conditions foreseen until the 1990s, it appears likely that the system will continue to be more "efficient" through adversity than it ever was during times of plenty. Improvement is always possible in the management of resources; higher education is not an exception. Neither should it be considered any less efficient than other public agencies or even large private corporations run by a self-perpetuating board of directors. Results of a system—not cost factors alone—should determine the efficiency of a system. By that criterion, the United States system is efficient.

FOOTNOTES

1. *Chronicle of Higher Education,* Volume XV, Number 6 (October 11, 1977), p. 5.
2. *Ibid.,* Number 11 (November 14, 1977), p. 20.
3. National Center for Educational Statistics, *The Condition of Education 1977,* Volume 3, Part One (Washington, D.C.: Government Printing Office, 1977), pp. 82-83.
4. *Ibid.,* p. 174.
5. *Ibid.,* p. 198.
6. United States Department of Commerce, Bureau of the Census, 1976, *Current Population Reports, Population Characters,* Table A, p. 1.
7. Alexander W. Astin, "The American Freshman Norms, Fall 1967," *Chronicle of Higher Education,* Volume XV, Number 19 (January 1978), p. 11.

8. *Ibid.*, pp. 12-13.
9. Glenny et al., *Presidents Confront Reality: From Edifice Complex to Universities Without Walls* (San Francisco: Jossey-Bass, 1976).
10. *Chronicle of Higher Education,* "Ladd-Lipset Survey," Volume XV, Number 11 (November 14, 1977), p. 2.
11. National Center for Educational Statistics, *The Condition of Education 1977,* Volume 3, Part One (Washington, D.C.: Government Printing Office, 1977), p. 123.
12. *Ibid.*, 1977, p. 122.
13. Howard R. Bowen, *Investment in Learning* (San Francisco: Jossey-Bass, 1977).
14. *Ibid.*
15. John W. Gardner, *No Easy Victories* (New York: Harper & Row, 1968), p. 65.
16. Allen Cartter, *Assessment of Quality in Graduate Education* (Washington, D.C.: American Council on Education, 1964); and Kenneth Roose, *A Rating of Graduate Programs* (Washington, D.C.: American Council on Education, 1969).
17. Patrick M. Callan, "Evaluation of Statewide Boards of Higher Education," paper presented at Kellogg/ECS Inservice Training Program, New Orleans, Louisiana, December 16, 1974, p. 13.
18. Lyman A. Glenny, *The Autonomy of Public Colleges: The Challenge of Coordination* (New York: McGraw-Hill, 1959).

SELECTED REFERENCES

BARAK, ROBERT J., AND BERDAHL, ROBERT O. *State-Level Academic Review in Higher Education.* Denver: Education Commission of the States for the Inservice Education Program, 1977.

BURN, BARBARA. *Higher Education in Nine Countries.* International Council for Educational Development. New York: Carnegie Commission on Higher Education, 1971.

EDUCATIONAL COMMISSION OF THE STATES. *The States and Graduate Education.* Report Number 59, 1975.

GLENNY, LYMAN A., BERDAHL, ROBERT O., PALOLA, ERNEST G., and PALTRIDGE, JAMES G., *Coordinating Higher Education for the '70s.* Berkeley: Center for Research and Development in Higher Education, University of California, 1971.

HODGKINSON, HAROLD L. *Institutions in Transition.* New York: McGraw-Hill, 1971.

MEDSKER, LELAND et al. *Extending Opportunities for a College Degree: Practices, Problems, and Potentials.* Berkeley: Center for Research and Development in Higher Education, University of California, 1975.

PALTRIDGE, GILBERT. *Self-Study Guidelines for Governing Boards for Public (Multicampus) Higher Education Systems.* Washington: Association of Governing Boards, 1977.

──────. *Self-Study Guidelines for State Postsecondary Education, Planning and Coordinating Boards.* Washington: Association of Governing Boards, 1977.

STATE HIGHER EDUCATION EXECUTIVE OFFICERS. "Major Issues of Concern to State Higher Education Agencies, 1977" for annual meeting at Big Sky, Montana, August 1-4, 1977. Mimeo.

THE CENTER FOR RESEARCH AND DEVELOPMENT IN HIGHER EDUCATION. *State Budgeting for Higher Education Series.* Berkeley: The Center for Research and Development in Higher Education.

>Glenny, L.A. et al. *Data Digest,* 1975.
>Schmidtlein, F.A. and Glenny, L.A. *The Political Economy of the Process,* 1977.
>Purves, R.A., and Glenny, L.A. *Information Systems and Technical Analyses,* 1976.
>Glenny, L.A. *Interagency Conflict and Consensus,* 1976.
>Meisinger, R.J., Jr. *The Uses of Formulas,* 1976.
>Bowen, F.M., and Glenny, L.A. *State Fiscal Stringency and Public Higher Education,* 1976.

THE CHRONICLE OF HIGHER EDUCATION.
Volume XV, Number 3, September 19, 1977.
Volume XV, Number 10, November 7, 1977.

UNIVERSITY OF MISSOURI. "The Report to the President of the University of Missouri" from the Task Force on State-Level Coordination and Governance of Higher Education, 1972.

DIRECTORS OF COUNTRY STUDIES

Australia
   Bruce Williams, Vice-Chancellor and Principal, University of Sydney.

Canada
   Edward Sheffield, Professor of Higher Education, Chairman, Higher Education Group, University of Toronto.
   Sponsor: Higher Education Group, University of Toronto.

Federal Republic of Germany
   Hansgert Peisert, Professor, Zentrum I, Bildungsforschung, University of Konstanz.
   Sponsor: University of Konstanz.

France
   Alain Bienaymé, Professor of Economics, University of Paris-Dauphine IX.
   Sponsor: Secretary of State for Higher Education.

Iran
   Abdol Hossein Samii, Director, Imperial Medical Center of Iran.
   M. Reza Vaghefi, Dean, School of Economics, University of Tehran.
   Sponsor: Reza Shah Kabir University.

Japan
   Katsuya Narita, Director of First Research Department, National Institute for Educational Research.
   Sponsor: National Institute for Educational Research.

Mexico
Alfonso Rangel Guerra, Programa Nacional de Superacion Academica, Secretaría de Educación Publica.
Sponsor: Asociación Nacional de Universidades e Institutos de Enseñanza Superior.

Poland
Jan Szczepanski, Professor, Institute of Philosophy, Warsaw.
Sponsor: Institute for Higher Education Research.

Sweden
Bertil Östergren, Adviser, National Board of Universities and Colleges.
Sponsor: National Board of Universities and Colleges.

Thailand
Sippanondha Ketudat, Secretary-General, National Education Commission.
Sponsor: National Education Commission.

United Kingdom
Anthony Becher, Professor of Education, University of Sussex.
Jack Embling, Former Deputy Under Secretary of State, Department of Education and Science.
Maurice Kogan, Professor of Government and Social Administration, Brunel University.
Sponsor: Leverhulme Trust.

United States
John R. Shea, Carnegie Council for Policy Studies in Higher Education.
David D. Henry, President Emeritus, University of Illinois at Urbana-Champaign.
Lyman A. Glenny, Center for Research and Development in Higher Education, University of California, Berkeley.
Sponsor: International Council for Educational Development.